Aimé Césaire

THE CARIBBEAN BIOGRAPHY SERIES

The Caribbean Biography Series from the University of the West Indies Press celebrates and memorializes the architects of Caribbean culture. The series aims to introduce general readers to those individuals who have made sterling contributions to the region in their chosen field – literature, the arts, politics, sports – and are the shapers and bearers of Caribbean identity.

Other Titles in This Series

AIMÉ CÉSAIRE

Elizabeth Walcott-Hackshaw

The University of the West Indies Press

Jamaica • Barbados • Trinidad and Tobago

The University of the West Indies Press
7A Gibraltar Hall Road, Mona
Kingston 7, Jamaica
www.uwipress.com

A catalogue record of this book is
available from the National Library of Jamaica.
ISBN: 978-976-640-829-9 (cloth)
978-976-640-830-5 (paper)
978-976-640-831-2 (Kindle)
978-976-640-832-9 (ePub)

Jacket and book design by Robert Harris
Set in Whitman 11.5/15

Printed in the United States of America

CONTENTS

PREFACE

Aimé Césaire introduced me to the literature of the French Caribbean. At the time, I was a graduate student at Boston University studying French literature in the true sense of the word, literature written by writers born in France. During my undergraduate years, I had studied many of the great names, the best of whom for me resided in the nineteenth century: Baudelaire, Flaubert and Rimbaud topped my list. My literary world at university, apart from these writers, also included writers from England and the English-speaking Caribbean. Although as a Trinidadian I had read Caribbean works at high school and on my own, my personal anthology was yet to include the great works of the French Caribbean and Haiti. I had heard of Césaire, but was formally introduced to him in a class on African literature that also included the Senegalese Léopold Sédar Senghor and Léon-Gontran Damas from French Guiana. All of these black writers were grouped under one umbrella as founding members of the Negritude movement. I quickly recognized and understood the sentiments in the poetry of both Senghor and Damas, but neither had the impact of Césaire's *Cahier d'un retour au pays natal*. The work resounded on many levels. I was a Caribbean student studying in a foreign country, missing my homeland and knowing that the ideas of what it meant to be black had never been clearer. Still, more than the invaluable ideas of Negritude, it was also Césaire's poetry that affected me and effected a personal *prise de conscience*. I reimagined the ways in which I saw the Caribbean in language and landscape.

During my qualifying examinations at the postgraduate level, I had another pivotal encounter with Césaire. For my qualifying exams, I was supposed to study a long list of writers from different centuries; I noticed that Césaire was not included on that list of great French writers from the twentieth century. I had no doubt in my mind that he deserved a place on that list, but in order for this to be done, I was asked to make a case before an examination committee. It must be said that this was still the mid-1980s and the metropolitan focus of my university was not uncommon among academic institutions at that time. Put it down to the bravery of youth, or the folly, but I remember the passion I felt in front of the committee, making my argument and believing that this was the most important thing that could possibly happen on that day. Césaire had to be placed on that list. What I remember was not my argument but my conviction. I was met with little resistance, just a few questions from a one or two professors and a small victory earned – Césaire's *Cahier d'un retour au pays natal* (*Notebook of a Return to My Native Land*) was included on my qualifying reading list. Jump ahead several decades later to my professorial inaugural lecture at the University of the West Indies, entitled "Cracks in the Edifice: Notes of a Native Daughter". Once again I drew from Césaire, and one of his students, Frantz Fanon, to help shape my argument. Both men from the French Caribbean island of Martinique had had a global impact on theories of race, identity, culture and politics. Both men had pointed to the cracks that existed in their time and, as I argued in that lecture, still exist today.

My small victory at university was a drop in an ocean of praise that has been bestowed on Césaire. His influence has been profound and pervasive; his ideas have been validated and contested. As a poet, playwright, essayist, theorist and politician he has left us with some of the most precious treasures: ideas and poetry. The conviction since my student days remains: Césaire's legacy is a part of our Caribbean heritage and is a necessary point of departure as we continue to grapple with who we are as a people in our young nations.

ONE

Aimé Fernand David Césaire grew up under French rule on the island of Martinique. He was born in Basse-Pointe, in the north of the island, on 26 June 1913. Césaire's father, Fernand Elphège Césaire, was a local taxation officer; his mother, Marie Félicité Éléonore, was a homemaker and seamstress. Césaire, the second of six children, had two sisters and three brothers. The first son of Éléonore and Fernand was Omer (1911), followed by Aimé (1913), Mireille (1915), Denise (1918), Georges (1922) and Arsène (1924). His paternal grandmother, Eugénie Macni, "la petite africaine", better known as Maman Nini, taught Césaire how to read and write by the age of four. He remembered her as a small woman with sparkling, intelligent and mischievous eyes. His grandmother played the role of confidante to her grandchildren and provided them with a moral compass to navigate the many dilemmas faced in their lifetime. The family's economic status was close to that of the rural poor and this encouraged them to place a high value on education, seeing it as a pathway to a better quality of life. Aspiring to a sound education was also due in many ways to Césaire's father and paternal grandfather. They were both ambitious men, and Césaire's grandfather, Nicolas Louis Fernand Césaire, had managed to become a schoolteacher and was promoted to the secondary school system even though he was born in 1868, a mere twenty years after the abolition of slavery by the French in 1848.

In 1913 the French Caribbean island of Martinique had 120,000 inhabitants. It was mostly rural and most people worked on the great sugar-cane plantations or the *habitations*. Slavery had not long been abolished; Césaire's great-grandparents (Maman Nini's parents) were enslaved people, freed before the abolition. Not long before Césaire was born, Saint-Pierre, the former capital, had been totally destroyed by the unexpected volcanic eruption of Mont Pelée on 8 May 1902. The tragic and horrific event killed close to thirty thousand people, making it one of the worst volcanic eruptions in history. The survivors, said to be no more than two or three, included a prisoner who had been locked away in solitary confinement in a stone cell when the volcano erupted, putting him in the safest place in the city. As a boy, Césaire would have heard many stories about the horrors of the eruption. It was only natural, then, that the metaphor of a volcanic eruption was later to take on a symbolic value in Césaire's poetic works. As he noted in a 1977 interview, "La Martinique est un pays montagneux et en même temps de feu . . . de feu à cause du soleil qui joue un très grand rôle dans ma poésie, mais aussi du volcan. . . . Car c'est précisément le volcan qui fait la liaison entre le feu et la terre, le feu et la montagne, le volcan n'étant que la montagne de feu, la montagne du feu" (Martinique is a country of mountains and at the same time of fire . . . fire because of the sun which plays a very important role in my poetry, but also of volcanoes. . . . Because it is precisely the volcano that creates the link between fire and earth, fire and mountain, the volcano being the mountain of fire, the mountain from fire).[1]

In 1924 Césaire's family moved to Fort-de-France, the capital of the French colony. The decision was made to ensure that the children could further their education. Éléonore used her skills as a dressmaker to help with the extra expenses. She attracted an elegant clientele and pedalled night and day on her Singer sewing machine at their new home at 100 Antoine-Siger Road. Césaire would later recall this image in his *Cahier du retour au pays natal*: "et ma mère dont les jambes pour notre faim inlassable pédalent, pédalent de jour, de nuit, je suis même reveillé la nuit par ces jambes inlassables qui pédalent la nuit et la morsure âpre dans la chair molle de la nuit d'une Singer que ma mère pédale, pédale pour notre faim et de jour et de nuit" (and my mother, whose legs pedal for our unflagging hunger, pedalling day and night, I was even awakened by these unflagging legs pedalling at night and the harsh bite into the soft flesh of night of a Singer that my mother pedals, pedals for our hunger night and day).[2]

For Césaire's generation, the only way forward was through industry at school; studying was always of primary importance. Césaire's father, Fernand, also understood that to benefit from a sound education, his children needed to master the French language. French colonial policy placed a high value on adherence to French cultural ideals and Fernand had ambitions for his children. He sent his daughters to the Pensionnat Colonial and the boys to the famous Lycée Victor Schoelcher, both in

Fort-de-France. Although initially Césaire was hurt by the harsh teasing he received from the other students at the school, particularly from those of the middle class, he quickly made a name for himself. His intelligence and application to his studies did not go unnoticed.

One of his fellow students at Schoelcher was none other than Léon-Gontran Damas, who had come from the French colony of Guyane, or French Guiana. The two would be reunited later on in their lives in Paris as founding members of the Negritude movement. Between the ages of eleven and fifteen, Césaire enjoyed and played team sports. In fact, he, along with Damas, organized two football teams at their school. Césaire's sporting activities did not affect his academic performance, in which he always excelled. He spent a lot of time in the library and often used his pocket money to buy books. Gilbert Gratiant, his English teacher, described Césaire as being gentle, pleasant and managing to do everything well.[3] This gentle tone, however, did not extend to his future works in both fiction and non-fiction, where he often expressed his frustrations and outrage at the harsh realities of racism and colonialism.

As a result of his brilliant academic performance, Césaire was awarded a scholarship in 1931, the same year he graduated from Schoelcher, to further his studies in Paris at the Lycée Louis-le-Grand. Césaire was eighteen when he left the island of Martinique for France aboard the ship *Le Pérou*. Many years later, when he returned to his home in 1939, he would be a different man, filled with an overwhelming passion and a desire to transform his homeland. His experience in the French metropole would be a turning point in his life, taking him towards fame as a great poet, politician and a transformative figure in the ideas of black consciousness. It was at the Lycée Louis-le-Grand that Césaire would meet his lifelong friend and co-founder of the Negritude movement, Senegalese poet Léopold Sédar Senghor. Césaire's elder by seven years, Senghor took the young Césaire under his wing. This friendship with Senghor had a profound impact on a personal level and awakened in Césaire a desire to claim his African identity. As he later said, "Quand j'ai connu Senghor, je me suis dit africain" (When I met Senghor, I called myself African).[4]

Césaire also met other young black students in Paris, including his old friend from the Lycée Victor Schoelcher, Damas. The opportunity to be admitted to one of the most prestigious institutions in France and finding himself among some of the most privileged students from elite French families was not lost on Césaire. Through hard work and a steely determination, he passed the highly competitive entrance examination to enter the prestigious L'École Normale Supérieure. At the institution, Césaire continued to devour works from the ancient classics to modern writers, from Sophocles to Marcel Proust. Of the French poets, he was particularly influenced by Arthur Rimbaud's *Une saison en enfer* (*A Season in Hell*). Césaire's breadth of literary influences was wide during this period; he was greatly influenced by other French literary giants apart from Rimbaud, including Mallarmé, Baudelaire, Lautréamont, Apollinaire and Claudel. He was also exposed to the works of African and black American writers who were part of the Harlem Renaissance, a prominent literary movement of the 1920s. The exposure to the works of these black voices made Césaire even more aware of the rich cultural heritage and commonalities that existed in the black world.[5] He came to realize that Martinique was more than a French colony, it was a part of the African diaspora.

It was no coincidence that all of these intellectuals and artists found themselves in Paris. Europe faced a turbulent time after World War I, and the French capital provided a unique creative space, with writers, artists and musicians from around the globe. It was the perfect environment for the convergence of ideas that would transform black identity politics forever. As a result of the exciting cultural interactions taking place in Paris, many American artists, both black and white, travelled to the capital. The writers of the Harlem Renaissance who had taken up residence in Paris to escape racism and segregation in the United States played a fundamental role in forming Césaire's ideas.

Exposed to such an environment, Césaire became intensely aware of his African heritage. He discovered the poems of Langston Hughes and Claude McKay published in the monthly bilingual journal *La revue du monde noir* (*Review of the Black World*). Both Hughes and McKay were key figures in the Harlem Renaissance. Hughes's syncopated jazz rhythms pushed the poetic form with his innovative structures. Jamaican-born McKay became one of the most militant voices of the Harlem Renaissance. The black francophone intellectuals in Paris could easily identify with these outcries against racial inequality that emanated from the Harlem Renaissance writers.

Paulette Nardal was among this group of influential thinkers. She was a chief editor of *La revue du monde noir*. Born in 1896 into the Martinican black bourgeoisie, Nardal arrived in Paris at the age of twenty-four after winning a scholarship to study at the Sorbonne. Paulette and her sister Jane were two of the first black women to be awarded a degree at the prestigious institution. Paulette's degree was in French and English. Of seven sisters, at least five of them were to receive degrees from the Sorbonne during the interwar period.[6] While in Paris, Nardal and her sisters organized cultural soirees at their apartment.

La revue du monde noir published six issues from 1931 to 1932. The bilingual review played a crucial role in allowing fellow black francophone writers to discover black writing from around the world. In reading the works of Claude McKay and Langston Hughes, Césaire could envisage the ways in which a greater literary space could be carved out for black cultural expression and ideas. This exposure was a motivating factor behind the journal *L'Étudiant noir* (Black Student) that he started in 1935 along with Senghor and Damas. *L'Étudiant noir* had as one of its pillars to articulate, reclaim and redefine black identity.

Paris, as the locus of ideas on black identity and pan-Africanism, facilitated their convergence and spread. This atmosphere inspired three young aspiring writers to envision what was possible in their poetics of engagement. Césaire, Damas and Senghor would do more than spread the word, they would give it a shape and a name. They understood the transformative power of poetics but also recognized the need to engage in political reform. The three shared a complex identity: they were black and French, but not born in France and yet part of the French colonial empire at that time. This setting away from their homes made them understand in a fundamental way the ambiguities of their French identity. They felt united in their desire to redefine their black experience through a rejection of

Western ideology that inherently saw blacks as inferior to whites. In their conceptualization of Negritude, Senghor, Damas and Césaire wanted to combat subjugation and reclaim the definition of what it meant to be black. Negritude was envisioned as a universal concept to include all people of African descent. Artistic expression of black culture was a major conduit through which this redefinition and revalidation was to take place.

Both Senghor and Césaire drew on their personal narratives and histories to define and express their visions. For Senghor, Negritude was a way to universally affirm the importance of African culture and, by extension, the black race. Africa symbolized the unifying motherland for all those Africans who had been brutally uprooted and dispossessed through the trade in enslaved people. The Negritude movement called for a cultural revolution placing Africa at the centre. If Senghor had a more universalist approach, with a view to giving those of African descent a sense of self and inheritance of a great cultural past, for Césaire, this idea of being African would have to be translated into his French Caribbean context. The complex notion of belonging was heightened while in Paris, where the question of their French identity was something they would have to come to terms with as well.

All three founding members of the Negritude movement would use their poetry to express this powerful new vision of black identity. Alongside their creative expression they also engaged in political activism. Senghor led his people to independence in 1960, became Senegal's first president and remained president for twenty years. Damas, author of the famous collection *Pigments*, was also involved in politics and was elected deputy for French Guiana from 1948 to 1951. Césaire too would go on to have a long political career that lasted for most of his life. His time in Paris was the foundation on which he built his later accomplishments. He went on to publish several poetry collections, plays and essays. His first major and most famous work, *Cahier d'un retour au pay natal*, published in 1939, was also a way, through the poetic imagination, to return to both Martinique and Africa.

While in Paris, Césaire was also attracted to Marxist ideals as articulated by Lenin and Stalin. Their radical rejection of capitalism and its exploitation of the proletariat drew many black artists and intellectuals to their cause. Césaire was attracted to Marxism's anticolonial sentiments, which coincided with his own ideas. Another major influence in Césaire's life during the interwar years was the surrealist movement. As with Marxism, the surrealist sentiment of revolt and rejection of rationalism in sociocultural contexts appealed to the young Césaire. Marxism and the ideology of the surrealist movement would influence his political views and his poetic works.

Paris also played a major role in Césaire's personal life; it was where he met his wife and mother of his children. When Césaire married Jeanne Aimée Marie Suzanne Roussy (also spelled Roussi) on 10 July 1937 in Paris, he was twenty-four years old and Suzanne was twenty-two. Césaire was in his second year of studies at the L'École Normale Supérieure. Also Martinican, Suzanne was intelligent, beautiful, well-educated and energetic, so much so that her maternal grandmother had given her the nickname Ti-Piment (Little Pepper). Césaire's sister Mireille played an important role in helping her brother meet his future wife in the French capital. Mireille and Suzanne had been class-mates in Martinique and both had gone to Paris to further their studies. It was while visiting his sister that Césaire met Suzanne. Mireille, who had recently arrived in Paris, was staying with Suzanne. Césaire fell for his future wife immediately, and not long after their first meeting they would be husband and wife. The young couple also did not wait long to start a family. Their first son, Jacques, was born in Paris on 9 May 1938. But, in spite of the joy that came from falling in love, getting mar-ried and the birth of his first child, this was a taxing period in Césaire's life.

The political climate in France and the world over was a tense one, with World War II fast approaching. Césaire acknowledged this difficult time in his life; he was faced with the demands of providing for a young family and the need to pass his exams. He was studying for a highly competitive examination, the agrégation, the highest qualification available for teachers at secondary level. Césaire would have to be successful in order to get a teaching post in France. He felt ill prepared and at that moment decided to return to Martinique. He did not take the agrégation, his final exam at the École Normale Supérieure, and soon made the decision to return to Martinique in order to create a more stable situation to provide for his family: "I was married, I had my child, life was very difficult for us."[7]

In August 1939, Césaire returned to Martinique with Suzanne and their son, Jacques, on board the *Bretagne*. The return voyage lasted two weeks. Their departure was well timed. In the fol-lowing month, on 3 September, France and Great Britain would declare war on Germany. Césaire and his family were among the last passengers on the *Bretagne*; they arrived in Fort-de-France in mid-September. On its return voyage to France, the *Bretagne* was torpedoed and sunk by the Germans.

Despite the political instability in France and around the world, this young generation of writers from Africa, Haiti, Martinique and French Guiana continued to publish poetry, essays and other works. It was also a productive creative period for the founding members of the Negritude movement. Damas published *Pigments* in 1937, a collection that was well received and included a preface by Robert Desnos, one of the leading French poets of the day. A year later, in 1938, Damas published *Retour de Guyane* (Return from Guiana). In 1939 Senghor published his classic essay "Ce que l'homme noir apporte" (What the Black Man Brings), in which he put forward the ideas of an egalitarian meeting between blacks and Greeks, emphasizing the humanist dimensions of Greek society, which had been influenced by African (Ancient Egyptian) society.

Between the time Césaire left Martinique and the time of his return, a transformation had taken place in him; the rebel had found a cause. He would devote himself to expressing his Negritude through his writings and eventually through actions in the cultural and political arenas. Césaire quickly found employment as a teacher at his old school, the prestigious Lycée Victor Schoelcher. One of his colleagues at that time was the poet René Ménil, who taught philosophy at the high school. Césaire taught Greek and Latin as well as contemporary and modern French literature. Some of the writers he exposed his students to included Malraux, Rimbaud, Lautréamont. He also introduced them to the surrealist poets and avant-garde writers such as

Jean-Paul Sartre and ensured that they were knowledgeable about African civilization.

A natural teacher, Césaire enjoyed bringing the many works to life in the classroom, well aware that he was influencing a generation of young thinkers. Many of the young bright minds would go on to critique or align themselves with Césaire's ideas. Either way, what mattered most to Césaire was the impact he could make on developing his students' intellectual capacity, giving them strong critical skills to analyse both the texts before them and the world outside the classroom. The high school had students who would also become famous, including Frantz Fanon and Édouard Glissant. Fanon, one of Césaire's students, would become a leading theorist on the politics of race, culture and identity. According to Césaire, he had moulded many young minds, some of whom had become friends; others, adversaries. But more importantly, he knew that he had influenced an entire generation.[8]

By 1939 he was already a published writer, with the first edition of the *Cahier* being featured in the little-known journal *Volontés* with the assistance of his professor, M. Petitbon, from the École Normale Supérieure.[9] During this period, he also wrote the long poem "Les pur-sang" ("The Thoroughbreds") and began work on his first play, *Et les chiens se taisaient* (*And the Dogs Were Silent*). His family was also expanding. Césaire and Suzanne had their second son, Jean-Paul, born in 1941 and named after Sartre. This tradition of giving his children the names of famous writers and intellectuals had already started with his first son, who was named after Jacques Rabemananjara, Malagasy politician, playwright and poet. His revolutionary protest writings include the poetry collection *Sur les marches du soir* (On the Edges of the Evening [1942]) and his play *Les dieux malgaches* (The Malagasy Gods [1947]) which embodied the sentiments of the Negritude movement. Another of their children, Michelle, was named after Michel Leiris, French surrealist writer and ethnographer.

Césaire's passion for starting literary journals did not end with his return to Martinique. In 1941 he, along with Suzanne and René Ménil, Aristide Maugée and other young Martinican intellectuals, launched *Tropiques*. Maugée had collaborated on the journal *L'Étudiant noir* in the mid-1930s in Paris and would go on to marry Césaire's sister Mireille, an English teacher. *Tropiques* was meant to fill what the founding members felt was a cultural void that existed on the island. The journal's editors wanted to foster intellectual, scientific and philosophical debate. They also wanted to provide a creative space for artists and writers to highlight their works. According to James Arnold, the literary magazine "spelled out very clearly the ideological connections between the evolving Martinican version of negritude and the culture of European modernism. Both biographically and in terms of cultural history *Tropiques* was a synthesis of the previous decade's accomplishment for Césaire."[10]

Five issues of *Tropiques* appeared between April 1941 and April 1942. The first issues sold for twelve francs a copy or forty francs for a year's subscription. But yearly subscriptions were rare, as readership was mostly composed of students. The funding for the review came primarily from the pockets of Césaire and Ménil. However, the conceptual shape of the review, with its subversive artistic politics, did not escape the Vichy officials on the island. Many of the island's bourgeoisie were also opposed to the ideas expressed in the journal. An inevitable and explosive standoff occurred in 1943 between the Vichy officials and the editors. On 10 May 1943, in a letter to Césaire, Lieutenant Bayle informed Césaire that he was forbidding publication of the review by withholding printing paper and accused the contributors of poisoning minds and sowing hatred. He also faulted the review for being "revolutionary, racial and sectarian". The laconic response to Bayle's letter came two days later on 12 May from the editors – Suzanne and Césaire, Georges Gratiant, Maugée, Ménil and Lucie Thésée. They answered each of Bayle's accusations, including the notion of racism, claiming that if they were in fact racists, it was the racism of Toussaint Louverture, Claude McKay and Langston Hughes rather than that of Drumont and Hitler. The sixth issue that had destabilized Bayle in such a profound manner included a piece written by Suzanne defiantly challenging the authoritarian state of affairs on the island and arguing that the surrealist ideas were in the service of liberty when in 1943 this very idea of liberty was under threat.[11]

This censorship was part of a harassment campaign by the Vichy authorities in their attempt to undermine the impact of the journal. The different editions of *Tropiques* spanned many areas: cultural, socio-economic, historical and psychological. Emphasis was also placed on the African diasporic community in America and its quest to claim and articulate its black identity. Césaire paid close attention to the works of the German ethnologist and archaeologist Leo Frobenius as well. Born in 1873, Frobenius introduced the term "Kulturkreis" or "culture circle", believing that all cultures grow and decline like organic life. Frobenius recognized African culture to be as significant as any other culture in human history, not a commonly held belief at that time.

It was only when there was a change in governance in 1943, when Governor Georges-Louis Ponton replaced Admiral Robert, that the ban on *Tropiques* was lifted. However, this was not the only avenue through which Césaire's works and ideas would reach the wider public. The New York review *Hemispheres,* under the direction of Yvan Goll, devoted a double issue to the French Caribbean (nos. 2–3, Fall/Winter 1943–44). This issue included "Un grand poète noir" ("A Great Black Poet") by the French surrealist poet André Breton. Césaire met Breton in 1941 when he was passing through Martinique, a meeting described by Césaire as one of the most important in his lifetime, as important as his meeting with Senghor more than a decade earlier.[12]

In 1944, on the invitation of Pierre Mabille, Césaire spent May to December of that year in Haiti. It was Césaire's first visit to an island that would come to have a profound impact on his vision of black aspirations and decolonization. Haiti's leaders like Toussaint Louverture served as powerful symbols of resistance and inspiration for Césaire's poetics and politics. Haiti symbolized both the black man's plight and his power to reclaim his Negritude. As Césaire wrote: "Haiti où la négritude se mit debout pour la première fois" (Haiti where negritude stood up for the first time) (*Cahier,* 24).

For the next ten years, Césaire's major works would be devoted to the question of Haiti's powerful and dramatic history, focusing on the revolutionary figures of Toussaint Louverture and Henri Christophe. Césaire's *Toussaint Louverture* (1960) explored the history of the Haitian Revolution, focusing on battles among white, black and mulatto, insurrections, and the black revolt that would eventually lead to the creation of the first black republic in the Western Hemisphere.[13] For Césaire, the Haitian Revolution was the embodiment of resistance, courage, sacrifice and hope, where a black nation was able to realize aspirations of equality.

While in Haiti, Césaire presented one of his most probing papers, "Poésie et connaissance" ("Poetry and Knowledge"), at the International Philosophical Conference in the capital, Port-au-Prince. Césaire's treatment of the subject provided invaluable insight into the relationship between the culture of modernism in Europe and the Negritude movement.[14] "Poésie et connaissance" would later be published in *Cahiers d'Haïti* in December 1944 and later in *Tropiques* in January 1945. Notably, the twelfth issue of *Tropiques* would be almost entirely devoted to Haiti. But 1945 was also the last year that *Tropiques* would be published. From then on, Césaire would be thrown into the political arena and would have to navigate his career as both writer and politician.

Césaire would come to dominate Martinican political life. In 1945, the same year that World War II came to an end, Césaire was first elected mayor of Fort-de-France, a position he would retain until 2001 with only one brief interruption. He was elected deputy to represent Martinique in France's National Assembly, where he served from 1946 to 1956 and again from 1958 to 1993. In 1945 he also joined the French Communist Party, the Parti Communiste Français. In the first elections of the post-war period, Césaire would become the representative for the colonial branch of the Stalinist political party. As one of many writers committed to the ideals of Marxism, he would later be disappointed by the realities of the party.[15] Césaire would eventually leave the party in 1956 and in 1958 would, along with his colleague and friend Pierre Aliker, co-found the Martinican Progressive Party. Aliker, like Césaire, would also give much of his life to public service, having held the post of deputy mayor of Fort-de-France for over forty years.

The move towards a political career may have been inspired by Marxist ideology, but it was equally motivated by Césaire's desire to effect change in his homeland. Césaire hoped that the concept and ideas of Negritude would inspire a *prise de conscience*. It was meant to encourage and promote pride in black culture and identity; as important for Césaire was to create better socio-economic conditions for poorer Martinicans. Césaire recognized the dialectical relationship between politics and culture: politics was simply one manifestation of an entire culture, and these two entities, politics and culture, created in Césaire's mind a historical synthesis.[16] For the other founding members of the Negritude movement, this dual vocation, combining poetics with political engagement, was an essential part of realizing change. Damas and Senghor, like Césaire, also entered the political arena as a way to realize sociopolitical equality in Senegal and French Guiana respectively. All three men represented their countries as deputies in the French National Assembly. Damas was a deputy in the French National Assembly from 1948 to 1951. In 1946 Senghor was also sent as one of two deputies to the National Assembly in Paris.

The year 1946 would be a pivotal one for the French colonies and in Césaire's political legacy. He would play a critical role in determining the political status and identity of his birthplace,

Martinique. The events of 1946 must be placed in the context of the post-war period. General Charles de Gaulle's attempt to recognize the contribution of the French colonies to the war effort promised greater rights and representations for citizens of the French Union, as it was to be called. But it was soon clear to all that there was no clear solution or path to greater independence. Nevertheless, the complex political context during the post-war period gave Césaire an opening to have the law of departmentalization proclaimed. He took advantage of the fact that the First Constituent Assembly was made up of a majority of socialist and communist representatives. This short-lived left-wing government pushed through a number of progressive laws related to colonial governance before it was dissolved in May 1946. Most important were the Houphouët-Boigny Act, which abolished forced labour in France's colonies, and the Lamine Guèye Act, which made citizens of France's colonial subjects. During this brief window of opportunity, Gaston Monnerville and Césaire managed to push through the French Assembly on 19 March 1946 the law proclaiming the "departmentalization" of France's *vieilles colonies*, including Martinique, Guadeloupe, French Guiana and Réunion.[17]

This was not an easy feat; the relationship between the colonies and France had always been ambiguous. During World War II, from 1940 to 1942, the Vichy regime ruled the island with an iron fist through the policies of Admiral Robert. The *békés*, or white minority on the island, for the most part supported the admiral's authoritarian rule, further alienating the black majority. However, Martinicans also had the example of the more liberal policies of de Gaulle. Both the repression of Robert and aspirations of de Gaulle informed the wider population's attitude towards departmentalization. The black majority wanted to have greater rights, especially when faced with the powerful socio-economic position of the *béké* minority. In many ways, the black majority identified with the humane principals and cultural aspirations of the post-war vision in France. Departmentalization was also seen as protection against the United States, the new post-war colonial power that the Martinicans associated with racism and the *békés*. The Americans were also keeping a keen eye on the political situation on the island, especially since the Martinicans had voted for an entire communist slate after the war. This had not gone unnoticed by the French and US authorities; they recognized that the island had in Césaire a brilliant thinker, an orator and a charismatic leader who had great appeal and influence over the population.[18]

Césaire, as deputy for Martinique, had found himself in Paris in 1945 to argue for better conditions for Martinicans in all sectors: agricultural, educational and, most importantly, political designation. The law of 1946 was meant to assimilate Martinique, Guadeloupe, French Guiana and the Indian Ocean island colony of Réunion into the *mère patrie*. It would make them fully fledged departments of France and, henceforth, they would have the same laws and rights applied to their peoples as to all other French citizens. Equality through assimilation was the main objective of departmentalization. Césaire's address on 18 September 1946 encapsulated the aspirations of Martinicans and by extension other countries in the French colonial empire. He argued that the French government could not have it both ways; it could not, on the one hand, build a democratic republic that strived to create racial equality and, at the same time, perpetuate a colonial system that continued to uphold racism, oppression and servitude.[19] Césaire's address was noted in the *La Marseillaise*. Commenting on the debates that were taking place and on the different contributions made by the delegates from overseas, the newspaper stated that the most impactful contribution came from Césaire. He was described by the paper as one of the best French poets and who, after this address, could now be counted as one of the best orators.[20]

The second National Assembly, after intense, acrimonious debate, decided to maintain the law of departmentalization but rejected the amendment to article 143 presented by Césaire in October 1946. This amendment afforded civil servants equal treatment and rights in the new departments to those enjoyed by the state and municipalities. Césaire was forced to modify his position as a result of the turbulent situation in France. In Martinique, unrest and strikes were paralysing the island. Georges Gratiant, who would be elected as the first president of the new General Council from 1946 to 1947, was arrested. The French gendarmes also arrested strikers and three deaths were recorded. Césaire expressed his profound disillusion with the idea of assimilation; to him it had failed. His speech on 4 May 1948 revealed his anger and frustration with the entire process. He characterized what was being offered as a mockery of what had actually been demanded: "l'assimilation que vous nous offrez aujourd'hui n'est qu'une caricature de celle que nous avons demandée".[21]

The ways in which colonial ideology was still influencing political, cultural and socio-economic conditions would later be powerfully expressed in Césaire's *Discours sur le colonialisme* (*Discourse on Colonialism*) written in 1950. Césaire's address at the Sorbonne on 27 April 1948, on the centenary of the abolition of slavery, would echo the same themes, ascribing a clear link from slavery to colonization. It was now clear to Césaire that the fight for equal rights in the French overseas departments or DOMs (Départements d'Outre-mer) would be a fight for decolonization. His verbal attacks against the French bourgeois also reflected a deep sense of betrayal that Césaire felt at this time.

In practice, the majority of laws and benefits from departmental status were not extended to the Antilles until well into the 1950s and 1960s, with many not being implemented until the 1970s and 1980s. Although these islands were certainly well-off in relation to some of the other Caribbean islands which had gained their independence from European colonial powers in the 1960s and 1970s, the overseas departments, despite the rhetoric of assimilation and equality, were much worse off in relation to France itself. Departmental status may have allowed some measure of political autonomy but the political policies of these islands, to this day, continue to be informed by the French government. The departments still rely on France for their economic survival. The French Caribbean islands' regional location, their colonial history and even the hardships encountered in the French metropolis have created an ambivalent and complex relationship with France. This relationship has shaped many of the cultural arguments and literary movements of the Caribbean region. Throughout his life, Césaire would face difficulties aligning his vision of Negritude and the realities of his role as a politician. Poetics and politics were not always easy allies. According to Arnold, his Negritude had to accommodate the dynamic political landscapes:

> His politics have appeared contradictory to some over a period of years. In 1946 he cosponsored the bill that transformed the Caribbean colonies into overseas departments of metropolitan France. In 1958 he gave last-minute support to De Gaulle's constitutional referendum on the Fifth Republic. . . . Since the founding of the PPM [Parti Progressiste Martiniquais] Césaire has favoured a qualified autonomy for Martinique. . . . Careful analysis of Césaire's concept of negritude shows that it bears no necessary relationship to any given political position, that it is, in short, a sociocultural ideology without a firm theoretical base. As such Césairian negritude has been at the mercy of shifting political conditions.[22]

Despite this critique, it is also important to see the evolution of Césaire's ideas in the context of his personal history. He would continue to fight for the rights of those he felt were oppressed throughout his career as both a politician and a writer. In this light, there was no contradiction.

TWO

Cahier d'un retour au pays natal is by far one of Césaire's most famous works. It contains seminal themes that he would explore in both his fiction and non-fiction throughout his lifetime. The long poem has acquired the status of a classic of black literature, becoming a symbol of the distinctive experience of black people in the modern world. The *Cahier* can equally be categorized as a classic of Caribbean literature in its quest to unearth the traumatic effects of slavery and colonization. Undoubtedly, as Abiola Irele contends, it is "the most impassioned statement of Africans and people of African descent, a sentiment deriving from their problematic historical relationship with the Western world".[23]

Césaire began to work on the poem in 1936 after a return trip from Yugoslavia with his friend Peter Guberina. Guberina would go on to write the preface to the *Cahier* in the definitive edition of the work published in 1956 by Présence Africaine. The evolution and various versions of the work trace Césaire's emergence as a major literary figure. The *Cahier* was first published in its entirety in the journal *Volontés* in August 1939. At the time, it was twenty-eight pages in length. There would be four incarnations before the poem took its definitive shape seventeen years later.

After the initial *Volontés* publication, the second version of the book was a bilingual edition published in 1947 in New York by Brentano, translated by Lionel Abel and Goll as *Memorandum on My Martinique*. This edition included Breton's now famous preface, "Un grand poète noir" ("A Great Black Poet"), which had been previously published in the special issue of *Hemispheres* that also featured Césaire's poetry and a full-page drawing by Afro-Cuban artist Wifredo Lam.[24] The second version of the *Cahier* had many changes and included a fragment from *Tropiques* (no. 5, 1942) entitled "En guise de manifeste littéraire" (In Lieu of a Literary Manifesto). On 25 March 1947, the same year that the bilingual edition appeared, the *Cahier* was published by Bordas with another illustration by Lam. The final and fourth version, modified from the third, was in *Présence Africaine*.

The *Cahier* in its many incarnations embodied the spirit of rebellion that the young Césaire felt at the time. He explored the poetic form, liberating himself from traditional poetic structures while acknowledging the influence of many great poets who had preceded him, including Baudelaire, Rimbaud, Mallarmé, Lautréamont, Péguy and Claudel. However, Césaire wanted to go beyond rebellion in form alone: he had a deep-rooted desire to create something new, akin to Rimbaud's *voyant*, giving the poet the power of a seer who could translate hidden meanings. Rimbaud, a surrealist before his time, articulated the difficult journey that the poet faced in his poem "Le bateau ivre" ("The Drunken Boat"). The poem captures the tumultuous movements from revelations to elation and, ultimately, disillusionment at the *voyant*'s inability to effect change. Similarly, the *Cahier* captures a turbulent journey of revelation, anger and disillusionment but ends, not with Rimbaud's despair but rather with the movement of ascent: "monte, Colombe / monte / monte / monte" (ascend, Dove / ascend / ascend / ascend) (64–65). This long poem was the manifestation of Césaire's desire to defy established norms in poetics and politics. No surprise that he was naturally drawn to Rimbaud and the surrealist concepts captured in Breton's anti-assimilationist, anti-traditionalist manifesto. Surrealism represented freedom from a past defined by hierarchical notions of race, class and culture; it was easy for Césaire to align his beliefs with those expressed by Breton. The members of the Negritude movement aspired to highlight the genius that existed in black writing through this new, avant-garde form; one that was scandalous to the French because it was so un-French. Surrealism, in Césaire's mind, was a welcome change and intersected with his desire to destroy or *dynamiter* traditional assimilationist ideas expressed under the cover of convention.[25]

The poetic value of the *Cahier* is undeniable, but the work also had a significant impact on the questions faced by those coming to terms with black, Antillean and French identities. The poem is one of the earliest manifestations of trauma poetics in Caribbean literature, exposing the effects of insidious racial trauma on the Caribbean psyche.[26] The *Cahier* is also an account of a poet's personal trajectory from self-hatred to self-acceptance. This poetic journey of trials echoes the Homeric arc of an Odyssean return. As with Odysseus, the poet must face his internal demons, which manifest themselves in different forms. These battles expose an ontological crisis and force the poet to plunge into the unknown. Césaire's surrealist aesthetics allows for this plunge into the darkest areas of his imagination. The onset of a journey is alluded to in the first words of the poem: "Au bout du petit matin" – "Foreday morning"[27] – a moment just before sunrise, just before the day begins. Before daybreak, the poet must face a tortured Antillean landscape described in the poem as traumatized, diseased, hungry, beaten and abused: "At the close of foreday morning, burgeoning with frail bays, the starving Antilles, the Antilles pockmarked with smallpox, the Antilles dynamited with alcohol, run aground in the mud of this bay, in the dust of this town ominously grounded" (*Journal*, 76–77).[28]

One of the most powerful scenes in the *Cahier* exposes the poet's fundamental traumatic struggle with his self-acceptance and Negritude. It is an inflection point that uncovers the poet's own cowardice. Facing his internalized self-hatred is the only path to true self-acceptance; it is a necessary stage in his path to recovering from a traumatic history of slavery and colonialism. In this scene, the poet-personage finds himself next to another black man in a streetcar:

> And I, and I
> > I who was singing with a clenched fist
> > You should know just how cowardly I was
> > One evening in a streetcar facing me, a *nègre*.
>
> A *nègre*,[29] big as a pongo,[30] trying to make himself small on the streetcar bench. He was trying to leave behind, on this grimy bench, his gigantic legs and his trembling famished boxer hands. And everything had left him, was leaving him. His negritude discoloured. . . . One could easily see how that industrious and malevolent thumb had kneaded bumps into his brow, bored two

bizarre parallel tunnels in his nose, over-exaggerated his lips, and
in a masterpiece of caricature, planed, polished and varnished
the tiniest cutest little ear in all creation.

He was a gangly *nègre* without rhythm or measure.

(*Cahier*, 40)

The poet tries to disassociate himself from this image and symbol of misery. He immediately adopts a racist gaze to distance
himself from the type of black image that he does not wish to
identify with; instead, he places himself in the personage of
an onlooker, othering this "symbol of misery". Through this
attempt at psychological realignment, the poet hopes to let the
others in the streetcar assume that his black identity is different
from this *nègre*; the poet wants them to know that he is closer
to their French values, culture, civilization and ideals of beauty.
In short, he wants them to know that he is more like them. The
result of the poet's desire to distance himself from this ugly
caricature of his Negritude is summed up in the line: "And the
whole thing added up perfectly to a hideous *nègre*." The women
on the streetcar were sneering at this black figure because, "Il
était COMIQUE ET LAID, COMIQUE ET LAID pour sûr (He was COMICAL
AND UGLY, / COMICAL AND UGLY for sure") (*Cahier*, 41).

No sooner does the poet align himself with the sneers and
mockery than he quickly acknowledges the shame he feels as a
result of his huge complicit smile, his "grand sourire complice".
He is well aware of his cowardice, fraudulent and disingenuous
stance as hero, saviour and voice of his people. He had proudly
proclaimed at the beginning of the *Cahier* that he would be the
voice of the people and of freedom; now he must confess that
his heroism is a farce ("Mon héroïsme, quelle farce!") (41). He

is no better than the people he has come home to save. This confession, a turning point in the *Cahier*, brings to light the harm done to marginalized groups by continuous exposure to ethnic stereotyping. The effect of this racism generates feelings of inferiority, inadequacy, and self-hatred. This insidious trauma can be passed on from one generation to the next.

Two concepts in this scene on the tramcar, COMIQUE ET LAID/ COMICAL AND UGLY, are taken from a poem by nineteenth-century poet Charles Baudelaire, entitled "L'albatros" ("The Albatross"). Baudelaire's poem also explores the notions of mockery, ugliness and the problematics of identity.[31] In the creative space, Césaire is a poet like Baudelaire, but on the ground, or on the deck of a ship, Césaire is a black man, mocked, like the albatross, like the *nègre* in the streetcar.

After this episode, Césaire's poet-personage can truly face the traumatic process of acknowledging and decolonizing his internalized colonial gaze. Only then can he say: "J'accepte . . . j'accepte . . . entièrement, sans réserve . . . ma race" (I accept . . . I accept . . . unconditionally . . . my race) (*Cahier*, 52). His Negritude must be without shame or exclusion, it must include the *nègre* on the streetcar. The encounter was a painful but necessary one, revealing the long, arduous process of self-decolonization.

The genius of the *Cahier* would help launch him onto the international literary sphere. Breton, who recognized Césaire as one of the greatest writers of their time, would help to catapult Césaire into that space. Breton was first introduced to the young poet on his trip to Martinique in 1941. Like many other intellectuals and artists, including Wifredo Lam, Breton was en route to the United States, leaving France as a result of the

German Occupation. France during the early 1940s was a divided country. Eric T. Jennings's significant contribution *Escape from Vichy: The Refugee Exodus to the French Caribbean* gives a vivid account of Vichy's discriminatory policies and attitudes towards the migrants in France and the role that the French Caribbean played as an escape avenue and venue for the European migrants during the period 1940 to 1941. According to Jennings, France's collapse at the hands of Germany in June 1940, and the chaos that ensued, further exacerbated the refugee crisis. France was unevenly carved in two, with an unoccupied zone (sometimes called the free zone) controlled by Vichy to the south, and a German-occupied zone to the north. Artists, intellectuals and writers like Sartre and Simone de Beauvoir left Paris to take refuge in the South of France. Although several thousand migrants may have reached the French Caribbean island of Martinique in 1940 and 1941, the vast majority of the endangered remained in France and met tragic ends.[32]

The Martinique route would eventually unravel in May 1941. However, between October 1940 and May 1941, fifteen ships left the Mediterranean port of Marseille for Fort-de-France. On one of these journeys from Marseille to Martinique, aboard the *Capitaine Paul Lemerle,* was some soon-to-be-famous "cargo" which included the anthropologist Claude Lévi-Strauss; the revolutionary Victor Serge; novelist Anna Seghers; painter Lam; surrealist poet Breton and his partner, artist Jacqueline Lamba, and their daughter, among many others. The harsh treatment of these passengers on their arrival in Martinique is described by Lévi-Strauss: "No sooner had we docked than (we were harangued) by an army possessed by a form of collective insanity.

. . . Those who were not French were called enemies; those who were French were stripped of their Frenchness through the accusation that they were cowards leaving their country." Breton corroborated Levi-Strauss's account, stating: "A very distinguished young scientist, called upon to continue his research in New York was told: *no you are not French, you are Jewish, and the so-called French Jews are worse for us than the Foreign ones.*"[33]

It was in this atmosphere of racist harassment and nationalism that Breton and Césaire met. Breton would later chronicle his time spent in the French Caribbean in the work *Martinique: Snake Charmer.* The title was taken from a 1907 painting by Henri Rosseau (known as Le Douanier) set in the tropics. There was no doubt that the Vichy officials were concerned about the connections that were being established between refugees and Martinicans, but although they were preoccupied with any anti-Vichy sentiment that could arise from these links, they did not foresee one of the greatest complicities – the intellectual exchanges between Césaire and Suzanne and surrealists like Breton.[34]

How Breton actually managed to "meet" Césaire is a story worth recounting, mainly because it was fortuitous. Breton, looking for a ribbon for his daughter, Aube, in a haberdashery, stumbled upon the inaugural edition of the journal *Tropiques*, printed in April 1941. The owner of the shop was none other than Martinican philosopher René Ménil's sister. Ménil, one of the co-founders of the journal, had met surrealists while in Paris in the 1930s. Breton and the group of refugee intellectuals, including Lamba, Lam and Helena Holzer (later Benitez), soon met up with the Césaires and spent long hours conversing in a bar in Fort-de-France. The exchanges that followed generated profound discussions and probing reflections on identity and race that would have a lasting impact on generations to come. Later, the Césaires took the group on a hike through the Absalon rainforest, an expedition that left an enduring impression on Lam, Breton and the Césaires. In 1942, Césaire wrote to Breton, saying, "We see the admirable Absalon valley only with and through you; it is one of the few parts of this land that is still bearable to me physically."[35]

Césaire would also benefit from Breton's presence on the island in the classroom. Édouard Glissant, thirteen years old at the time, although too young to be in Césaire's senior class, still remembered these classes convening with Breton in 1941. No doubt, it would have been a coup for any teacher to have the grand master of the surrealist movement in person before a class of students. The effect that this meeting with Breton had on Césaire's life was comparable to his relationship with his close friend Senghor. Breton and Césaire would remain friends ever after. They shared common ideological goals: to revolt against the established orders of cultural, racial and social hierarchies that fostered oppression. Two of Césaire's most influential friendships, with Breton and Senghor, had an effect on the way Césaire saw the world, but he would equally affect theirs.

Although critics like James Arnold credit Breton for giving Césaire an international literary presence,[36] others, like Alvan A. Ikoku, believe that the ties between these two intellectuals proved mutually beneficial. Césaire had found an influential champion and platform through his friendship with Breton, but the latter also found a new face for his divided surrealist movement, weakened in part by his departure from Marseille, which some of his comrades considered desertion.[37] The relationship between Negritude and the surrealist movement could be seen in the editions of *Tropiques*: some of the articles referenced Breton and his movement, while two dealt specifically with the work of Lam. *Tropiques*' table of contents was also influenced by Afro-American, Cuban and Hispanic literature, but it was concerned most of all with the question of locating Martinican identity within black, French and African contexts. Both Césaire's Negritude and the freedom afforded it in surrealist poetics encouraged him to explore and excavate the authentic Martinican self. In a 2002 interview, Césaire recalled this important period in his life: "I said to myself; let's throw away everything conventional, . . . the Martinican imitations of French literature. . . . Let's toss all that out! Dig into yourself! Go on, dig deeper and deeper! And when you have dug enough, you'll find something. You'll find the foundational black."[38]

In the United States, Breton became very active in the literary scene in New York, and in 1943 he published Césaire's "Tam-Tam (II)", a poem dedicated to the Afro-Cuban artist Wifredo Lam. When Breton died in 1966, Césaire, in a moving homage, lamented having lost someone who since their meeting had always been a part of his life and had changed it in a decisive manner.[39]

Lam, one of the travellers from Marseille to Martinique, was another important figure in Césaire's life. Their lives also intersected in other ways: both men were of Afro-Caribbean origin and were grappling with ways to express in their art their complex colonial histories. Lam was born in 1902 in Sagua la

Grande, Cuba, to a mother of African–Spanish origin and a Cantonese immigrant father. He studied art at Havana's School of Fine Arts and later went to Madrid, where he briefly studied academic painting. In 1936 and 1937, Lam fought on the Republican side in the Spanish Civil war. In the 1920s, Lam's work reflected the influences of the Madrid school and Henri Matisse. However, after 1936, he was heavily influenced by Picasso's technique and African art. African art was popular during the 1930s in Paris, especially among the surrealists. When Lam fled Barcelona for Paris in 1938, he became friends with his mentor, Picasso. Through Picasso, Lam met several members of the avant-garde and began to experiment with many styles, moving towards modernism and experimenting with cubism. After meeting Breton, Lam began to experiment with surrealism and became an active member of the movement.

Although Lam only spent approximately forty days in Martinique, his stay on the island had a profound impact on the painter. Meeting the Césaires and the rest of the members of *Tropiques* was a pivotal moment in Lam's artistic development. *Tropiques* published the first-ever sustained and enthusiastic article on Lam's work in 1943, after Lam had already left Martinique. The Cuban painter was also particularly captivated by Césaire's *Cahier d'un retour au pays natal*, as was Césaire with Lam's rich Afro-Caribbean allegories and references. In Lam, Césaire saw a proponent of "poetic *marronage*" and a guiding beacon of freedom for the Caribbean.[40] At first, they were drawn together by their shared Afro-Caribbean vision and desire to probe the effects of colonialism on the cultural landscape, but soon they also formed a close friendship.

The meeting with Césaire, coupled with Lam's return to the Caribbean region, had a profound influence on his work. One of his most celebrated pieces, *The Jungle,* may have been influenced by his time in Martinique and the hike he took with Césaire and Suzanne as well as other members of the group. According to his then-spouse Holzer, "During this outing [to Absalon], Wifredo and I came to appreciate for the first time the structure and character of a virgin forest – the jungle."[41] Both ideas and images would have come together in the location of that "jungle". Art historian Robert Linsley characterized Lam's work as "an alchemical mixture of Third World liberation, Surrealism, and Negritude". Linsley argues that Lam's work can best be understood in the context of Negritude.[42] Both Lam and Césaire would have to grapple with the historical trauma of two colonial regimes: Spain in the case of Lam and France for Césaire. Their parallel visions were to come together in 1943, when Lam illustrated the Spanish translation of Césaire's *Cahier.* Lam would also publish a large portfolio of prints in collaboration with Césaire in 1945 in the review *Cahiers d'art,* numbers 20–21. Césaire and Lam shared a similar path filled with contradictions in their search for authenticity in their personal lives, in their art and in their return to their native land. They were also connected in their desire to express these contradictions in their life's works.

On the occasion of the centenary of France's abolition of slavery in 1948, a now famous anthology devoted to black and Malagasy poetry was edited by Senghor for the Press Universitaires de France. The anthology included the poetry of Césaire, Senghor and Damas as well as the works of David Diop, Étienne Léro, Jean-Joseph Rabearivelo and Jean-Fernand Brierre. Senghor asked Sartre to write the introduction to the anthology. This soon-to-be-influential piece of writing was entitled "Orphée noir" ("Black Orpheus"). Senghor admired Sartre's philosophical prowess and shared many of his political ideas. Senghor also knew that Sartre would be able to draw a global audience, exposing them to the works of these black poets and to the Negritude movement.

In his preface, Sartre described the poetry in the anthology as "orphique", referencing its power, beauty and persuasive quality, perhaps just as Orpheus's musical gifts persuaded Pluto to allow Eurydice to leave the underworld. Sartre's "Black Orpheus" carefully dissected these poems of revolt and reclamation. He paid particular attention to Césaire's expression of the role that Negritude played in redefining black identity through the reaffirmation of African cultural heritage. Sartre noted in his preface that the question of subjugation was not limited to the black race. This sentiment had also been expressed in the *Cahier*, where Césaire himself had identified with the oppressed:

> As there are hyena-men and panther-men, I would be a jew-man,
> a kaffir-man,
> a hindu-man-from-Calcutta,
> a Harlem-man-who-does-not-vote.[43]
>   (*Journal*, 93)

Another question that Sartre brought to the fore was the connection between racial inequality and the economic struggles of the proletariat. This was also something that Césaire himself would later explore in *Discours sur le colonialisme* (*Discourse on Colonialism*). Sartre advanced a phenomenological argument focused on the ways in which the Jew, simply as a result of his skin colour, could advance further than the dark-skinned Negro:

> A Jew, white among whites, can deny that he is a Jew, can declare himself a man among men.
>
> The Negro cannot deny that he is a Negro nor claim for himself that abstract colorless humanity: he is black. Therefore he is driven toward authenticity: insulted, enslaved, he stands up, he picks up the word "nigger" that they had thrown at him like a stone, he asserts his rights as black, facing the white man, with pride. The final unity that will draw all oppressed people together in the same combat must be preceded by what I call the moment of separation or of negativity: this antiracist racism is the only road that can lead to the abolition of racial differences.[44]

Sartre's interpretation of the Negritude movement in "Orphée noir" impacted the ways in which the movement was interpreted by Sartre's own readers and, according to James Arnold, influenced the way in which Césaire was read. Yet, for all its good intentions to bring to the fore the movement's powerful impact on reimagining the place of black culture and identity, it can also be argued that "Orphée noir" ironically fell into some of the traps of exoticism and essentialism that Sartre himself critiqued, giving the "Negro" stereotypical attributes of "fecundity", "rhythm" and an essential "black soul".

Sartre believed that black artistic expression was a revolutionary weapon against European class, racial and economic oppression. His philosophical arguments and battles for decolonization allowed him to forge ties with Césaire and Fanon. Sartre remained engaged in the battle against alienation and marginalization. In the aftermath of World War II, Sartre, like many writers and intellectuals of the time, would interrogate and expose the traumatic effects of anti-Semitism, racism and inequality in his work.

Apart from Césaire, Sartre formed ties with many others in the Negritude movement and was a member of the editorial and patronage committee for the first issue of the journal *Présence Africaine*, started in Paris by Alioune Diop in 1947. The original patronage committee for the journal also included Senghor, Emmanuel Mounier, Paul Rivet, André Gide, Albert Camus, Michel Leiris and Richard Wright. Césaire was in charge of international publications on the committee. In the first issue of *Présence Africaine*, Sartre published an article entitled "Présence noire" ("Black Presence") in which he argued against tokenism and advocated for a genuine black presence in European social and intellectual life. Sartre believed that tokenism was simply a way to expiate the guilt of a closed European society.[45] These thematic concerns would remain with Sartre throughout his career as he battled against marginalization, xenophobia and economic oppression.

In 1950 Césaire, at age thirty-seven, began six very productive years both in his political and his writing careers. His family with his wife Suzanne had expanded as well, and he was now the father of six children: Jacques, Jean-Paul, Francis, Ina, Marc and Michèle. He had clear political goals; of primary importance was to ensure that the law of departmentalization was enforced and applied in the French overseas departments. This goal, however, would prove to be a challenge throughout his political career. As a writer, his international fame grew, aided by the support that he gained from Breton and Sartre.

Césaire wrote several collections of poems around this time. *Les armes miraculeuses* (*The Miraculous Weapons*) came out in 1946; the poems from this collection were first published in *Tropiques* between 1941 and 1945. The influence and experimentalist approach of the surrealists were even more pronounced in these poems. The poems were less rhetorical than those in the *Cahier* but the forceful sentiments of revolt remained. Cultural awakening, resisting and opposing colonial regimes like those of Admiral Robert would remain major tropes in Césaire's works. The *Cahier* had described a journey that focused on Negritude ideals of reclaiming and reaffirming black identity; *Les armes miraculeuses* refracted the harsh realities that the Martinican faced under the Vichy regime. The modernist techniques in *Les armes miraculeuses* attracted immediate attention from critics in Paris. Many praised the primacy given to the botanical imagery of the poems, while others criticized the collection's angry, vehement tone. Roger Garaudy's article entitled "Aimé Césaire: Poète de la colère" (Aimé Césaire: The Angry Poet) appeared in *L'Humanité* on 24 August 1946; the article did not hesitate to praise Césaire's talent but it also criticized the poet's tone.[46]

In 1948 Césaire published another collection of poetry, *Soleil cou coupé* (*Solar Throat Slashed*). Many of the poems from *Soleil cou coupé* would be included and added to those of *Corps perdu* (*Lost Body*), published in 1949, and finally in the collection *Cadastre* (*Cadaster*) in 1961. The poems in *Soleil cou coupé* and *Corps perdu* are as hermetic as those of *Les armes miraculeuses*. The title *Soleil cou coupé* was taken from the last line in the first poem, "Zone", from Guillaume Apollinaire's *Alcools* published in 1913. Césaire recognized Apollinaire as one of his literary ancestors. "Zone" captured the transcendent quality that resonated in Césaire's work and his ability, like Apollinaire, to combine ancestral and modern motifs in both form and content. In "Zone", Apollinaire discarded the use of punctuation and used both "tu" and "vous" to address himself. His poetic devices signalled his desire to break with traditional forms to create a new way of imagining the present yet inviting re-examination of the past. These nonconformist sensibilities appealed to Césaire and his nostalgia for a past that recalled the greatness of the African people, similar to the Old World–New World dynamic that Apollinaire wrestled with.

Global occurrences, particularly incidents of injustice, would become part of Césaire's corpus. In the 1950s, France would see many anticolonial uprisings taking place throughout the French colonies. On 30 January 1950 in the Côte-d'Ivoire, in Dimbokro and Yamoussoukro, there were twelve deaths and at least fifty wounded. These events led Césaire to write "Le temps de la liberté" ("The Time of Freedom") first published in *L'Humanité* in 1950 and reprinted in Russian translation in Moscow's *Literaturnaya Gazeta* and later in his collection *Ferrements* (Irons) published in 1960. "Le temps de la liberté" described and memorialized this violent, bloody time as the "la saison du soleil rouge" (the season of the red sun). *Ferrements* would go on to win the René Laporte prize in 1960. It revealed once again the surrealist influence in Césaire's work but, as with his other works, this influence was also a means to an end. As the title indicates, the poems evoke the horrific conditions of slavery and colonialism. Still, there is the overarching desire to find ways to escape from these iron bars (*ferrements*), to move beyond a past marked by suffering and, instead, to find hope and freedom.

The challenges that Césaire expressed in his poetry resonated both collectively and personally. The 1950s and 1960s were a time of rebellion and revolt for the colonized nations of the world. Césaire's personal life was also going through a turbulent period. In 1963 he and Suzanne would divorce. The two had collaborated on many projects; Suzanne played an important role in the journals *L'Étudiant noir* and *Tropiques*. She published many of her own essays in *Tropiques*. In these essays, Suzanne recognized the value of European literary legacies but saw the dangers in assimilation and emphasized, instead, the need for autochthonous literature. She was able to envision a multi-ethnic, multicultural composition in the Caribbean and the fundamental need to re-examine and uproot deeply embedded destructive self-perceptions of black identity.

Martinican author Daniel Maximin's collection of essays written by the Césaires when the couple worked on *Tropiques* captures many of Suzanne's innovative ideas. In *Le grand camouflage: Écrits de dissidence (1941–1945)*, Maximin describes Suzanne's essays as among the greatest and most luminous texts on Antillean identity, placing them in the company of those expressed by Fanon in *Peau noire, masques blancs (Black Skin, White Masks)*.[47] The title essay, "Le grand camouflage" ("The Great Camouflage"), was written in 1945. In that essay, Suzanne described the extraordinary day when the two Césaires, in April of 1942, walked through the Absalon forest near the Mont Pelée volcano with the refugee intellectuals.

Many critics have noted the key role played by Suzanne in

shaping the political and theoretical orientation of *Tropiques*. Suzanne may well have been ahead of her time, as Anny Dominique Curtius notes, when it came to her ecopolitical awareness, which went beyond "the notion of exotic wanderings, the purity of nature, and romantic reverie". Suzanne's work brought a unique and powerful literary consciousness to the questions of land exploration, dispossession and disempowerment, or what Curtius describes as the "early Edenic appropriations of the Caribbean". The extract illustrates Suzanne's vision of a new way of writing and seeing, moving away from the sentimental towards a more modern empowering eco-poetics: "Come on now, real poetry lies elsewhere. Far from rhymes, laments, sea breezes, parrots. Stiff and stout bamboos changing direction, we decree the death of sappy, sentimental, folkloric literature. And to hell with hibiscus, frangipani, and bougainvillea. Martinican poetry will be cannibal or it will not be."[48]

Apart from her probing and provocative essays, she wrote and produced a theatrical adaptation of Lafcadio Hearn's *Youma: The Story of a West-Indian Slave* (1890) entitled *Youma, aurore de la liberté* (The Dawn of Liberty).[49] Suzanne Césaire, mother, writer, activist and scholar, contributed in no small way to the poetic vision of *Tropiques* and to Caribbean literature as a whole. She died a few months before her fifty-first birthday on 16 May 1966 after a long illness.

The personal tragedies were not the only dramas taking place in Césaire's life at this time: he would also make a pivotal decision to resign from the French Communist Party. Césaire had been a member of the party since 1945. For Césaire, the party was an embodiment of the rights and dignity of all men without regard to race, religion or colour. In 1953, along with other members of the Parti Communiste Français, he attended Stalin's funeral in Moscow. He would write to his Martinican comrades about his time there, describing it as enriching and exciting, noting that one of the most memorable experiences was meeting Maurice Thorez, secretary general of the French Communist Party. As Césaire declared, "J'ai passé en tout sept jours en URSS. Ça a été une des semaines les plus riches que j'aie jamais vécues"[50] (I spent seven days in all in the USSR. It was one of the most extraordinary weeks of my life). However, less than two years later, in an open letter to Thorez, Césaire would resign from the same French Communist Party that once held his high esteem.

The letter to Thorez dated 24 October 1956 outlined Césaire's reasons for leaving the French Communist Party ("Pourquoi je quitte le PCF"). His discontent with the actions of the Stalinist regime was made clear. However, Césaire's growing discontent with the party was also based on its inability to privilege the project of decolonization. The idea that the party espoused notions of European cultural superiority was profoundly objectionable to Césaire. He accused the party of sharing the bourgeois ideal of the superiority of Western culture.[51] Césaire was not renouncing the ideals of Marxism or communism but the manner in which the ideology was being applied when it came to black people: "What I am renouncing is the way in which some have used Marxism and communism. What I want is that Marxism and communism be used to serve black people, not black people used to serve Marxism and communism."[52]

Many of these frustrations had been expressed earlier in his influential pamphlet *Discours sur le colonialisme*, first published in 1950 by Éditions Réclame and five years later in *Présence Africaine*. In a rebellious tone, the *Discours* presented an incisive, classic polemical argument against the enduring traumatic effects of colonialism on both the colonized and the colonizer. Césaire's ideas could have easily inspired the nationalist wave in French African literature during the 1950s, particularly the works of Mongo Béti, Ferdinand Oyono and Ousmane Sembène. The polemics in *Discours*, as with his letter to Maurice Thorez, set up a clear dichotomy between colonization and civilization. Europe, according to Césaire, could not be defined as civilized, with its horrendous, indefensible treatment of the areas of the world that Europe colonized in the name of civilization. False, hypocritical equations were also propagated in the name of civilization: "*christianisme = civilisation; paganisme = sauvagerie*" (*Discours*, 8).

For Césaire, there was a direct link between the cultural situation of black artists and the history of colonial domination. This was a subject he explored in his address "Culture et colonisation" ("Culture and Colonization") delivered at the Premier Congrès des écrivains et artistes noirs (First Congress of Black Writers and Artists), organized by *Présence Africaine* at the Sorbonne in 1956. In the address, Césaire argued that to restore order to the cultural chaos that existed, black voices needed to reclaim their place in the theatre of history.

Césaire's *Cahier* was an early expressions of revolt and rebellion; it recorded a personal journey of awakening, illumination and affirmation of his Negritude. His vision also included the disenfranchised as a result of a shared colonial past. From the 1950s onward, his voice was decidedly one of collective rebellion and decolonization. In Césaire's mind, there were still too many countries in the world whose people still suffered under the yoke of colonial systems. The ideas expressed in *Discours sur le colonialisme*, "Lettre à Maurice Thorez", and "Culture et colonisation" gave voice to what would also be his continuing and lifelong battle for justice.

THREE

Throughout his life, Césaire assumed active roles as both a politician and writer, but he did not believe that creative work should be prescriptive or be given parameters predetermined by political responsibilities; artistic freedom was always necessary. In "L'homme de culture et ses responsibilitiés" (The Man of Culture and His Responsibilities), an address delivered at the Second Congress of Black Writers and Artists in Rome 1959, Césaire presented this notion. Black culture had a role to play in hastening the decolonization enterprise; this was not a messianic quest, but something that could be achieved by the simple act of creating works and giving form to artistic expression. He argued that colonial regimes engaged in socio-economic and cultural colonization by colonizing ideas, privileging colonial expression and perpetuating a master-enslaved, creator-consumer dynamic. Works and ideas that challenged colonial domination and effected a *prise de conscience* were powerful weapons against the trauma of colonization. These works could also have an impact on psychologically dismantling the inferiority complex that colonizers tried to instil in the colonized psyche. Césaire felt that artists should be allowed to express these injustices without censure.

This desire to promote the ideas of decolonization took shape in the political and artistic arenas throughout Césaire's life. These philosophical debates and injustices were also explored on the stage in his theatrical productions. The theatre allowed Césaire's anticolonial sentiments another space to give voice to his beliefs. His first major production, *Et les chiens se taisaient* (*And the Dogs Were Silent*) was first published as a dramatic poem included in *Les armes miraculeuses* (*The Miraculous Weapons*) in 1946, but was republished ten years later, in 1956, as a full play. This marked a crossover from the poetic to the theatrical treatment of Césaire's ideas and, as with his other plays, permitted a more public and direct transmission of his works and opinions.

Et les chiens se taisaient is perhaps one of Césaire's most lyrical plays, the first in a series of plays exploring the fate of black leaders faced with impossible choices. *La tragédie du roi Christophe* (*The Tragedy of King Christopher*) was more widely performed and had greater success than *Et les chiens se taisaient*. *La tragédie du roi Christophe* was written for the Salzburg Festival in 1964 and was also performed in Venice, Brussels and Berlin during the summer of 1964. It would later be performed at the Arts Festival in Dakar in April 1966 and in Montreal in 1967.

As the title indicates, the play was inspired by the history of the Haitian Revolution. Henri Christophe was a dramatic, if complex, symbol, both for the role he played in Haitian history and the lessons that could be gleaned from his life. These lessons were especially important when faced with the risks and possible pitfalls that awaited the newly free states of black Africa in the 1960s. The play begins with the assassination in 1806 of Jean Jacques Dessalines, who, with the proclamation of Haitian independence on 1 January 1804, had declared himself emperor under the title of Jacques I. Dessalines also ordered the systematic massacre of the whites on the island. *La tragédie du roi Christophe* would not be Césaire's only creative exploration of the victories and tragedies of the Haitian Revolution. He would return to this problematic of power to show how ideals of equality and humanity could fall prey to the tragic flaw of hubris. Through his writings on Haitian leaders, Césaire would try to understand this drive for absolute control and the ways in which authentic humane values became corrupted time and time again.

However, one figure stood out from the rest for Césaire. Toussaint Louverture's role in the Haitian Revolution as a symbol of black empowerment and pride influenced and inspired Césaire's anticolonial vision. Apart from including the figure of Toussaint Louverture in his poetic works, most notably in his *Cahier,* Césaire would go on to write a biography of this fascinating historical figure in 1960 entitled *Toussaint Louverture: la révolution française et le problème colonial* (Toussaint Louverture: The French Revolution and the Colonial Problem). *Toussaint Louverture* afforded Césaire the opportunity to probe the question of colonization within the context of the French revolutionary ideals of liberty, equality and fraternity. Leading the Haitian people, Toussaint Louverture had managed to defeat Europe's powerful armies and its colonial aspirations, making Saint-Domingue the first country in modern times to challenge European domination.

These powerful anticolonial aspirations and actions made him an inspirational symbol for many pan-African countries.

Une saison au Congo (*A Season in the Congo*), published in 1966, was another theatrical work that revolved around the question of revolutionary awakening, liberation and the dangers of absolute power. The play looked even more closely at these themes explored in the two earlier plays, *Et les chiens se taisaient* and *La tragédie du roi Christophe*. *Une saison* is a depiction of the Congo rebellion in 1960 and the last months of Congolese political leader Patrice Lumumba's life before his assassination. And there was no question of the political lessons that are meant to be gleaned from these plays; Césaire's experiences had taught him that hunger for change had to be combined with a clear vision of the way forward. There was no question of the didactic quality of these plays, portraying through these complex leaders the political lessons to be gleaned from their decisions.

Une tempête (*A Tempest*) written in 1969, inspired by William Shakespeare's *The Tempest*, was produced by Césaire in collaboration with the French theatrical director Jean-Marie Serreau. The play was originally written for the International Cultural Festival in Hammameth, Tunisia, in 1969. For Césaire, as for many other writers from the region, Caliban had become an important figure through whom ideas of colonization and civilization could be explored. Several writers from the English and Hispanic Caribbean used this symbolic character in their works. Barbadian writer Edward Kamau Brathwaite published *Islands* in 1969, a poem dedicated to Caliban. Cuban writer Roberto Fernández Retamar also saw Caliban as a powerful metaphor and revolutionary symbol for the Caribbean. George Lamming, in his collection of essays *The Pleasures of Exile*, published in 1960, drew on the personage of Caliban to explore the effects of colonization. Césaire was not alone in his desire to offer radical rereadings of this enigmatic figure and to relocate Caliban in *Une tempête*. It was a way, as for his fellow Caribbean writers, to undermine the dominant savage-enslaved versus civilized-master dynamic. When the play was first performed in England at the Gate Theatre in London, it was received with wide acclaim and described not simply as a rereading of the play but as an original and powerful work. Césaire presented Prospero as a totalitarian figure with an absolute will to power. Prospero was not forgiving, but rather represented cold reasoning: he was a portrait of the so-called enlightened, rational European with a cold reasoning that had led to oppressive, totalitarian regimes. The play was an example of the "civilized" European coming face to face for the first time with an unknown world of magic and difference. This master-enslaved, civilized-uncivilized dynamic remained a dominant theme that Césaire would pursue in his works and battle against throughout his lifetime.

However, despite his desire to fight for the rights of those who had unjustly suffered as a result of oppressive regimes, decisions that Césaire had made earlier in his life seemed at times to go against these ideals and would haunt him throughout his political career. One such decision was his support of departmentalization. From as early as 1950, it was evident to Césaire that the hope he had for economic development as a result of departmentalization in the French overseas territories would not come to pass. Césaire based his decision on the belief that the DOMs would have had more to gain if they stayed tied to France. He did not see the possibility of economic viability without maintaining this relationship. His hope was that the overseas territories would have been given greater autonomy, releasing them from the stronghold of the metropole. Césaire would have to acknowledge his intention did not result in his desired outcome. Decolonization was always a part of Césaire's aspiration and mission for the French Caribbean islands. These ideas were clearly stated in "Décolonisation pour les Antilles" (Decolonization for the Antilles), an article published in *Présence Africaine*. His words also translated into action when he founded the Parti Progressiste Martiniquais six months after he resigned from the Parti Communiste Français. Until his death in 2008, Césaire maintained a devoted following of members of the Parti Progressiste Martiniquais. He also started *Le progressiste,* a newspaper meant to sensitize Martinicans to local and global issues of the day, particularly those that had a direct impact on their lives. But the battle for greater autonomy faced by the DOMs would always be linked to his past political decisions.

Césaire's activism and writings affected many beyond his immediate world, but world events also had a profound and lasting impression on him. The Algerian War of Independence was such an event that drew attention once again to France's colonial domination. As a member of the action committee against the Algerian War (other members included François Mauriac and Sartre), Césaire was well aware of the occurrences and consequences of the battles being waged by the Algerians against the French.

Both Césaire's and Sartre's speeches against France's colonial actions were published in April 1956 in *Temps modernes*. Césaire argued that Martinique as well as Algeria should be free from the yoke of colonization. The seriousness of the situation in Algeria brought to the fore the question of decolonization for all of the French territories. De Gaulle knew that what was happening in Algeria could spread like a contagion to other French territories. As a result, he sent André Malraux to Guadeloupe and Martinique in 1958 to meet with Césaire. Around the same time, Fanon, one of Césaire's old students at the Lycée Victor Schoelcher, was meeting Sartre for the first time in Rome at the Second Congress for Black Writers. Fanon had just completed *Les damnés de la terre* (*The Wretched of the Earth*) and he had always been a great admirer of Sartre's ideas in "Orphée noir". It was no surprise, then, that Fanon would ask Sartre to write the preface to *Les damnés de la terre*. The book, published in 1961, shortly before the end of the Algerian War, was an unbridled account of Fanon's political ideology. Sartre saw in Fanon what he had already seen in Césaire, a new revolutionary writer.

The Algerian War of Independence started in 1954 as the National Liberation Front had sought, through guerrilla warfare, diplomatic recognition at the United Nations and the desire to establish a sovereign Algerian state. After the brutalities and the ferocity of the fighting in the "Battles of Algiers" in 1956–57, de Gaulle declared in 1959 that Algerians had the right to determine their own future. An agreement was finally signed in 1962, when Algeria became independent. Sartre had already stated clearly while at a conference in Rio de Janeiro in 1960 that there was only one solution for Algeria and that was the right to self-determination. The Algerian War added fire to the desire of both

Césaire and Fanon to expose the exploitative relationship that existed between Martinique and France, particularly as it related to decolonization, self-determination and greater autonomy.

At the Second Congress of Black Writers, Césaire framed his argument around a cultural imperative, emphasizing the role of black intellectuals in articulating the process of decolonization and reconstruction of a cultural identity. He stressed the importance of making those of French Caribbean heritage see themselves in a new light by recognizing their identity apart from being French. Césaire believed that writers had a role to play in creating this sociopolitical and cultural awareness.[53] In his speech, he affirmed his duality as poet and politician as he focused on the Antillean condition. The problems faced in his *pays natal* had always been of primary concern for him, but his profound disappointment with the French Communist Party, the failures of departmentalization and, in more recent times, the brutalities of the Algerian War intensified his impetus to create better conditions for the French Caribbean territories. He pointed to the sociopolitical inequalities in the Caribbean and reaffirmed the importance of local culture and traditions. Nomenclature was part of this process of cultural reclamation; it was important to name things that were Martinican by their Martinican name. Writers, artists, intellectuals had a mission to hasten the process of decolonization and to ensure that it was an effective and lasting decolonizing effort. Their role was to highlight critical moments in the history of the oppressed and to motivate them to find courage to advocate for self-determination. Césaire described writers as not only engineers of the soul but also the propagators, the multipliers of souls and, to a certain extent, the inventors of souls: "Nous sommes des *propagateurs d'âmes*, des multiplicateurs d'âmes, et à la limite des *inventeurs d'âmes*."[54]

Although Césaire drew a direct link between the politics of engagement and his own poetics, he also acknowledged the individual's right to the freedom of creative expression. He recognized the value of the local language in his decolonizing project and emphasized the importance of Creole as part of Martinican identity. Cultural engagement, socio-economics and political participation were all part of the same equation for Césaire. He was not alone in his view of the writer's role in society. Sartre had similarly pleaded for a literature of engagement in 1945 and, like Césaire, shared in the belief that the writer was part of the society to record both the reverberations and the silences.[55]

The more localized focus did not take away from Césaire's vision of the important contribution of African culture and traditions in the formation of Antillean identity. Such validation was the foundation of his Negritude. Still, the movement's ties to African culture had always faced many critics along the way who felt that its Afrocentric parameters excluded the cultural diversity of the Caribbean region as well as other colonized Creole-speaking regions. In time, the three founding members – Césaire, Senghor and Damas – would face complex political issues at home and that would force them to recontextualize what Negritude meant at particular points in their lives.

In a 1971 interview with Lilyan Kesteloot, Césaire repudiated Senghor's political and cultural position, without actually mentioning him by name: "I am for negritude from a literary point of view and as a personal ethic, but I am against an ideology founded on negritude." There would come a time when Césaire and Senghor would have clearly divergent views on their vision of Negritude. The Negritude movement envisioned in Paris in the 1930s with Damas would have to transition into the socio-economic and political context they faced in their different countries. Senghor and Césaire were both black men, but they were from different worlds. Césaire's experience in the French Caribbean was not the same as Senghor's in Africa. As Césaire would tell Kesteloot: "All of us blacks have our own countries, and I am an Antillean now."[56]

The question of culture for Césaire, and more specifically black culture that drew from and took pride in its link to Africa, outweighed the notion of a black essence. He could not accept what he saw as Senghor's biological essentialist reading of what it meant to be black.[57] For Césaire, Negritude could not promote the notion of exclusion; it was not meant to be alienating, but rather a way to embrace all the oppressed in the name of humanity. His focus on Antillean Negritude went hand in hand with his growing decolonizing project. Apart from the Algerian War, other uprisings on the African continent shed more light on his own situation in the French Caribbean. The unfulfilled promises of departmentalization coupled with harsh socio-economic conditions and the insensitivity of the French authorities created a climate of frustration in Martinique. Césaire had originally hoped that President de Gaulle would give the overseas departments more autonomy without the heavy-handed control of previous French governments. Malraux's visit to Martinique was meant to reassure Césaire of de Gaulle's good intentions for the island and of the president's plan to review articles of the constitution relative to the status of the DOMs, giving them more control over their socio-economic development. But the confidence that Césaire initially felt was soon undermined by the events that followed.

Although the Parti Progressiste Martiniquais enjoyed support from the Martinican population, as seen in the municipal elections on 8 March 1959, there was evidence of growing unrest in the capital, Fort-de-France. Three young Martinicans lost their lives at the hands of the police. At a time when the island was in mourning for this loss, Césaire was in Paris for his parliamentary duties. Although he was criticized for his absence, Césaire returned to his home as quickly as possible. The riots of 1959 led to a seismic shift in the social, political and racial climate on the island, driving Césaire to assert that the December uprisings and the tragic events that followed were proof that Martinique was still a colonial country and that colonialism was alive and well: "Ce que les événements de décembre révèlent c'est notre pays est encore un pays colonial et que le colonialisme n'est pas mort."[58]

The fact that so many of the former British colonies were moving towards further autonomy and independence had not escaped Césaire. But even after the uprisings in Martinique, the French government acceded no concessions to quell the discontent and so it continued to grow. In March 1961 in Carbet, three agricultural workers were killed during a strike: Suzanne Marie-Calixte, Marcelin Laurencine and Édouard Valide. The situation was also deteriorating in Guadeloupe and French Guiana. In an article published in *Le Monde* in March 1961, Césaire spoke of the crisis in the overseas departments and the oppressive colonial system that was perpetuated by departmentalization. His speech at the town hall in Fort-de-France on 11 April 1961 also characterized the efforts of the French government as discriminatory, oppressive and colonizing. Césaire was still not seeking independent status but rather greater autonomy for the DOMs. He did not want to cut off ties with France, believing that the effect would be detrimental to the Martinican economy, but he insisted on giving Martinicans the opportunity to freely manage their own affairs: "Je ne dis pas que la Martinique doit se séparer de la France. Je dis que dans un ensemble français, en parfaite solidarité avec la France, les Martiniquais doivent gérer librement leurs propres affaires."[59] Césaire also maintained that a colonizing mentality towards the DOMs still existed in the French government.

The oppression and inequality that led to these uprisings were confirmed in a study commissioned by UNESCO in 1958 on the problems of "minorities in the New World". The authors of the study concluded that black Martinicans, although they constituted the overwhelming majority on the island, were considered a "minority" as a result of racial discrimination and lack of economic power:

> It would seem doubtful then that we could consider the people of color in Martinique as a minority group. Yet, not only are they, as a group depressed economically, but their Negroid physical characteristics (or the memory of a Negroid ancestor) remain as a symbol of slave status and as a barrier to their complete assimilation into French national society. . . . Taken as a group, however, the people of color of Martinique, like many minorities throughout the world, form a majority in numerical terms.

There was a pervasive practice of colourism on the island that made the "mulatto" population seem more French. In fact, the educated mulattoes were more French than the French themselves, priding themselves on polished Parisian accents and elaborate figures of speech. The mulattoes' armour against colour prejudice was these refined manners and educated speech.[60]

These notions of departmentalization and decolonization have always been complex issues for the Antillean population, tied to a history of racism, colourism and French cultural inheritance. Césaire understood the complex nature of these dynamics. As Kristen Stromberg Childers argues, "In their desire to be fully embraced by the French nation, Martiniquans identified two distinct Frances: one ideal republican, and grantor of liberties, represented by Charles de Gaulle; the other, a France of white racist *békés* working in league with the United States."[61] This complex idea of what it meant to be black and French was something Césaire grappled with throughout his tenure as a political representative of the Martinican people.

During this period of the 1960s and 1970s, there was also a dual migration taking place. Martinicans were moving to France and those from the French metropole were migrating to the French Caribbean. The desire to live in France was primarily due to the limited opportunities for employment in French Caribbean departments. On the other hand, many French families from the metropole installed themselves in the French Caribbean islands because they saw opportunities seemingly unavailable to the locals. Césaire characterized this movement as a form of genocide by substitution. The emigration of the Antilleans and immigration of the Europeans created what Césaire referred to in his annual contribution at the National Assembly in France in 1977 as "L'Europe tropicale". For him, it was simply another way to recolonize these territories.[62]

In 1962, the year when Algeria finally gained its independence from France, Césaire took this as yet another opportunity to advocate for political decolonization of the Antilles. He continued to focus attention on the punitive measures taken by French authorities against the protests in Martinique. On 10 May 1963, in *Le progressiste,* addressing the conseil général de la Martinique and to the Ministre de Départements d'outre-mer, Césaire focused on the harsh treatment meted out to a group of students whose scholarships were taken away because they had signed a petition against the arrest of militants from a young anticolonialist Martinican organization, the Organisation de la jeunesse anticolonialiste de la Martinique. Césaire's public outcries against the authorities did not go unnoticed and he would face threats to his own personal safety. These threats did not stop him from speaking out against the injustices being committed against those advocating an end to oppressive colonialist policies.

In 1963 Césaire met with representatives of political parties from the four overseas departments Martinique, Guadeloupe, French Guiana and Réunion, each country advocating for more autonomy as repressive measures continued in Martinique and Guadeloupe. The younger generation in particular were less willing to accept the status quo and there was a growing call for more autonomy and for independence from France. Despite the cries for independence, Césaire maintained his stance for greater autonomy rather than total independence. He held to the view that independence was economically unrealistic and could lead to dire consequences for the French islands. His battle to decolonize the departments would continue, but within the framework of autonomy.

When the newly elected president Valéry Giscard d'Estaing visited Martinique in 1974, Césaire invited him to city hall, but, unlike his predecessor de Gaulle, d'Estaing turned down the invitation. The snub by d'Estaing reflected the tension that now existed between the metropole and the French departments. In another incident, Senghor, in his capacity as president of Senegal, wanted a theatre troupe from Dakar to perform *La tragédie du roi Christophe* in Fort-de-France. Senghor was on an official visit to Haiti and felt it would be a great opportunity to bring this play, written by his old friend and performed by African actors, to Martinique. However, the prefecture refused the applications for visas for the African actors. Senghor threatened to cancel his trip if the actors did not get their visas, and only then did the prefecture agree.

In 1978, a year filled with more political uprisings and violence, Césaire lost his long-time friend Léon-Gontran Damas. The poet, diplomat and cultural theorist had played a crucial role in the vision of Negritude; he was among the first writers of his generation to address the psychological impact of internalized self-hatred. His first poetry collection, *Pigments*, brought to the fore the psyche of the colonized. These were difficult days for Césaire: he had lost a dear friend and there was a growing divide in the Martinican population between those who wanted greater autonomy and others seeking complete independence from France.

At the beginning of the new decade, there was some hope

that the return of a socialist government in France would bring change to the status and power of the DOMs. With this in mind, in 1981 Césaire gave his support to the new president, François Mitterrand. Césaire also pressed for greater decentralization of powers, giving the departments more administrative autonomy for economic development. Gaston Defferre, the interior minister at the time, supported this policy of greater autonomy through decentralization for the French municipalities and the departments. A response came in what would be known as Les lois Defferre (the Gaston Defferre Laws) in 1982. These decentralization measures, the first of their kind, were among the most important reforms of the new Mitterrand presidency.

Even though there were steps towards greater autonomy in the last decades of the twentieth century, the departmental status remains a problematic situation for the French Caribbean islands in the twenty-first century. Although departmentalization may have raised the standard of living in the French Caribbean territories as compared to some of the other independent nations in the Caribbean, it also created a dependency dynamic that remains fragile to this day. The influx of capital from France and a higher standard of living than in most of their Caribbean neighbours have weakened the local economy and created the illusion of wealth. There remains a serious unemployment problem, creating further polarization between racial groups. This dependency syndrome further undermines the sense of a local cultural identity.[63]

In 2008, the year of Césaire's death, the world faced a global financial crisis that created even more uncertainty for the DOMs and their dependency on European financial stability. The status of the relationship remains uncertain, since it is possible that the DOMs may become too financially burdensome for the French economy. Yet the complicated situation for the departments in the French Caribbean was always more than a question of greater socio-economic and political control. Race, culture and ideology have always been seminal issues to be addressed. The question of identity within the context of their ties to France and their geographical location in the Caribbean have always played a role in the ways in which those from the DOM have been seen and how they see themselves. The real battle would take a psychological war to decolonize pervasive and powerful notions of European cultural superiority. Fanon had made this argument throughout his life, echoing Césaire's determination to break the master-enslaved, colonizer-colonized cycle. Fanon refused to be a prisoner of his past. He rejected a polarized vision that set up binaries of little value where essentialized black values and ethics were pitted against essentialized white values and ethics. Fanon promoted, like Édouard Glissant, a notion of "endless self-creation". In 1961, Fanon lost his battle with cancer, but his fellow Antilleans, like Césaire and Glissant, continued Fanon's desire to expose the deep-seated problem of self-definition. Glissant and Césaire may have mapped different routes, but they recognized in their poetics and politics that the way forward meant having to come to terms with being black, French, Caribbean and European, colonial subject and postcolonial citizen.[64]

Césaire's long and impactful political career spanned generations. He was only thirty-two years old in 1945 when he was first elected mayor of Fort-de-France and a representative to the French constituent assembly. He held on to the mayoral office for the next fifty-six years. In 1946 he was elected deputy for Martinique to the National Assembly in Paris, a position he would hold until 1993. Much of his life had been spent serving his country and leading it through some of the most significant political changes and social unrest. Césaire held firm to his belief that complete independence from France was not the solution for the French Caribbean islands. He advocated and fought for departmental status, but was decidedly and profoundly disappointed by the slow-moving improvements that he had envisioned with the DOM status. The system of government remained too centralized and the subsidies were not adequate to allow for any major changes in infrastructural development on the island that would lead to better living conditions for the Martinican people. Césaire argued for increased autonomy but felt strongly that the DOMs, for their economic survival, needed to maintain linkages with France through a departmental relationship.

As a result of his convictions, Césaire faced harsh criticism from those who advocated independence. Glissant, an *indépendentiste*, was one of his harshest critics when it came to what Glissant saw as the only way forward – Martinican independence. He felt that dependence on France stymied not only political self-determination but also cultural aspirations of a Martinican identity. His concept of *Antillanité*, or Caribbeanness, provided the antidote to assimilationist ideas; it went beyond the static parameters of an Afrocentric definition of Caribbean identity. Glissant felt that such a definition proposed by the

Negritude movement did not allow for the dynamic, ever-changing nature of identity. Any definition of Caribbean identity would have to include the multicultural, multi-ethnic nature of the region, reflecting both similarity and difference. Identity for Glissant was also relational; it was important to look both inwards and outwards to see the region in a global context.[65]

In 1981 Glissant's *Le Discours Antillais* (*Caribbean Discourse*) was the first of what would be several theoretical works on the complex identity problematic that faced the region. Glissant's ideas were taken up by the Créolistes: Patrick Chamoiseau, Jean Bernabé and Raphaël Confiant. They acknowledged their debt to Césaire, stating they were forever Césaire's sons: "Nous sommes à jamais les fils de Césaire." Like Glissant, they did not think that Negritude, although it had played an important role in restoring and rehabilitating black identity, sufficiently addressed the multicultural Caribbean mosaic. The Créolistes, echoing Glissant's sentiments, felt that Negritude's Afrocentric vision was too limiting and did not reflect the diversity and heterogenous identity of the Caribbean region. Their manifesto *Éloge de la créolité* (*In Praise of Creoleness*) was first published by Gallimard in 1989 and in English translation in 1990 in the journal *Callaloo*. *Éloge* was dedicated to Césaire, Édouard Glissant and the Haitian writer, painter and activist Frankétyèn. The importance of the Creole language and the mission of the Créolistes to insist on its inherent cultural value as a marker of one's identity is in the inclusion of Frankétyèn, born Franck Étienne in 1936. His novel *Dézafi* was the first to be written and published in Haitian Creole, in 1975. He is known as the father of Haitian letters. The Créoliste manifesto begins with a dramatic declaration: "Neither Europeans, nor Africans, nor Asians, we proclaim ourselves Creoles."[66]

Glissant and the Créolistes differed sharply from Césaire in their sociopolitical and cultural vision of Martinique. Nevertheless, they also recognized Césaire's undeniable contribution and commitment to the region, and most notably his gifts as a poet. In his moving homage to Césaire, Glissant wrote the following about *Cahier d'un retour au pays natal*:

> composed during the French Resistance and amongst the greatest poems of our age, one which for me carries a deeper meaning well beyond its reputation as a work of political militancy . . . Aimé Césaire's poetics is one of volcanoes and eruptions; it is torn from the tangles of consciousness, sailing the waves coursing out of black suffering; with at moments a surprising tenderness of spring water and a clamor of joy and jubilation.[67]

In 1982 Césaire published his last collection of poetry, *moi, laminaire . . . (I, Laminaria)*. Written over a period of twelve years, the poems recall similar themes to past collections, but the proclamations found in the *Cahier*, his first collection, are replaced by interrogations and self-doubt. If the *Cahier* announced the beginning of a difficult journey, *moi, laminaire . . .* finds the poet at the end of this voyage. But, typically of Césaire, he is not afraid to expose the difficult truths as he reflects retrospectively and introspectively on his life as a poet and politician.[68] He also recalls the loss of dear friends in his elegies to Damas and Fanon. The title of the collection is also significant: laminaria, a brown alga commonly known as kelp, is found in the Pacific and Atlantic oceans. This tangled forest of kelp beds is also part of the Caribbean seascape. Through his ecological identi-

fication and the poet's metamorphosis into different animals
and elements, he reaffirms one of his most enduring ideas, our
interconnectedness:

> Miguel Angel immergea sa peau d'homme
> > et revêtit sa peau de dauphin
>
> Miguel Angel dévêtit sa peau de dauphin
> > et se changea en arc-en-ciel
>
> Miguel Angel rejetant sa peau d'eau bleue
> > revêtit sa peau de volcan
>
> et s'installa montagne toujours verte
> > à l'horizon de tous les hommes
>
> (Miguel Angel submerged his human skin
> and put on his dolphin skin
>
> Miguel Angel took off his dolphin skin
> and changed into a rainbow
>
> Miguel Angel casting off his skin of blue water
> put on his volcano skin
>
> and took his place an evergreen mountain
> on the horizon of all mankind)
> > (*moi, laminaire . . .*, 79)

Some have seen Césaire's politics as a contrary to his poetics,
especially since his writings consistently expressed his determination to decolonize both cultural and political arenas. In
the *Guardian*'s obituary of the poet-politician, James Ferguson

reinforced these accusations of contradictory impulses: "The contradictions at the heart of Césaire's career remained unresolved. Despite the massive importation of French consumerism into Martinique, he continued to argue that cultural autonomy could co-exist with departmentalisation. And despite the development of Martinique as a distant outpost of the EU, he persisted in looking to Africa as the source of authenticity."[69]

Glissant offers a response. For him, Césaire's poetics and politics were part of the same equation, each supporting the other. They were part of two trajectories through which Césaire could articulate and act on his beliefs.[70] Additionally, the political battles Césaire waged were not detrimental to his poetic production; in fact, each side, politics and poetics, enriched the other. His fiction and non-fiction were spaces that allowed him to work through questions that had no easy solution. If Césaire's vision is to be interpreted by some as contradictory, it remained a consistent contradiction, a constant process of honest intellectual reflection and evolution. He worked through the difficulties he saw facing his homeland in the public political arena and in the more private world of his poetic imagination. He did not live with any illusions about the sacrifices or the complexity of his reality. Césaire and Glissant, two formidable Martinicans, shared a profound desire to refute the vestiges of colonization in its many forms and to present possible, if different, routes towards overcoming the effects of a history of domination. The *Cahier* introduced the world to one of the greatest poets born in the Caribbean archipelago, and Breton was not alone in recognizing this work as a masterpiece.

Césaire will be remembered for many things: as a political

activist who, right or wrong in his convictions, through failures and successes, always fought for those who had been wronged by the vestiges of colonial regimes. He was engaged in a decolonizing battle that lasted throughout his long career as a writer and politician. When he stepped down from the French National Assembly in 1993 and as mayor of Fort-de-France in 2001, his service to his country had lasted most of his life. To honour this lifelong commitment to his country, the airport in Le Lamentin, a suburb of the capital, Fort-de-France, was renamed the Aimé Césaire International Airport in 2007.

On 9 April 2008, Césaire was admitted to the Pierre Zobda-Quitman hospital in Fort-de-France. The nonagenarian was said to be suffering from serious heart problems. His hospitalization made both local and foreign news; Martinicans were anxious to know the fate of "Papa Césaire", as he was fondly called. It would not be too long before the world would learn of his death on 17 April 2008. Césaire was given a state funeral three days later at the Pierre Aliker Football Stadium. Thousands of Martinicans, young and old, filled the stadium on that day, along with local, regional and foreign dignitaries, including French president Nicolas Sarkozy.[71] Pierre Aliker gave a moving tribute to his friend, eulogizing on the ways in which Césaire had changed the face of Martinique. The sentiment of love and commitment to his country would be echoed by Césaire's daughter, ethnologist and playwright Ina Césaire, who believed that the love her father held for his country could be found in all of his works ("Toute l'oeuvre de mon père est contenue dans l'amour pour son pays"). Césaire's body was laid to rest at the La Joyau cemetery in Fort-de-France. By a presidential decree of 17 March

2011, a ceremonial plaque in Césaire's honour was unveiled at the Panthéon in Paris, where celebrated French writers like Jean-Jacques Rousseau, Victor Hugo and Émile Zola had been laid to rest in its necropolis.

Césaire once declared in a 1982 interview with Daniel Maximin[72] that he had always been fascinated by trees; this vegetal motif was central to him. His favourite tree was the *fromager*, a kapok tree. He would love to take walks to the top of a hill where he could see the Caribbean Sea to his right and the Atlantic to his left; there he could find his favourite tree with its spreading branches and the fallen leaves on the path. Nature in all its forms interested Césaire. In his poetry, from the *Cahier* to *moi, laminaire . . .*, he explored natural metaphors that were often tied to human nature. In his politics he fought for the rights of his own people and for all those who had been oppressed. In his writings he sought to understand the effects of cultural domination. As he said in an interview with Guadeloupean writer Maryse Condé, "La culture, c'est tout ce que l'homme a inventé pour rendre le monde vivable et la mort affrontable" (Culture is what man invented to make life tolerable and death bearable).[73] Many who met Césaire described him as small in stature but formidable in character. He was, as with all poetic geniuses, a complex individual with a voice that could erupt like a volcano or soothe like the *fromagers* he so loved. His influence and ideas went beyond the Caribbean Sea and beyond the Atlantic, inspiring writers and artists from around the globe, including the likes of Sartre, Breton and Lam. He was a literary father, a father to his country and a voice of the colonized.

Césaire laid the foundation for the Caribbean region's sociocultural, political and psychological decolonization. During his lifetime, he crafted necessary and provocative debates about black Caribbean identity. His piercing observations are still alive today in global movements compelled to insist that black lives matter. Césaire wanted those of Afro-Caribbean heritage to take pride in their black heritage, to claim their Negritude and never be ashamed of that image of the *nègre* on the streetcar.

NOTES

Unless otherwise noted, all translations are my own.

1. Césaire, "Interview", 1.
2. Césaire, *Cahier*, 18. This and all books by Césaire are hereafter cited in the text using short titles.
3. See Arnold, *Modernism*, 7.
4. For more on Césaire's early life and a close reading of *Cahier d'un retour au pays natal*, see Irele, "Introduction", 7.
5. See Toumson and Henry-Valmore, *Aimé Césaire*, 40.
6. For more on the role of the Nardal sisters and the role women played in the Negritude movement see Sharpley-Whiting, *Negritude Women*.
7. See Toumson and Henry-Valmore, *Aimé Césaire*, 68.
8. Césaire: "J'étais professeur. Je faisais un cours de littérature pour une classe de première. . . . J'avais des disciples. C'était très important. J'ai formé des quantités de jeunes gens qui sont maintenant des hommes – certains sont devenus des amis, d'autres des adversaires, enfin peu importe. J'étais professeur, assez efficace, semble-t-il, et j'ai eu incontestablement de l'influence sur toute une génération." Ibid., 73.
9. See Irele, "Introduction", 18.
10. See Arnold, *Modernism*, 13.

11. Ibid.
12. Toumson and Henry-Valmore, *Aimé Césaire*, 76.
13. Arnold, *Modernism*, 14.
14. Ibid., 13.
15. Ibid., 14.
16. See Toumson and Henry-Valmore, *Aimé Césaire*, 82.
17. See Nesbitt, "Departmentalization", 32.
18. For more on the complex situation that existed at the time between France, the French colonies and America, see Childers, "Citizenship", 2.
19. Césaire: "Vous voulez édifier une république démocratique, une république sociale, une république qui n'admettra aucune distinction de race et de valeur et, en même temps, vous essayez de conserver, de maintenir, de perpétuer le système colonialiste qui porte dans ses flancs le racisme, l'oppression et la servitude?" Toumson and Henry-Valmore, *Aimé Césaire*, 85.
20. "La plus marquante de ces interventions fut sans doute celle de M. Aimé Césaire, député communiste de la Martinique. On savait . . . qu'il comptait parmi les meilleurs poètes français. Il se révéla comme un de nos meilleurs orateurs." Ibid.
21. Ibid., 87.
22. Arnold, *Modernism*, 15.
23. Irele, "Introduction", 1.
24. See Rosemont and Kelley, *Black, Brown, and Beige*, 203.
25. See Toumson and Henry-Valmore, *Aimé Césaire*, 98.
26. The analysis of this pivotal scene in the *Cahier* is also discussed in my professorial lecture (Walcott-Hackshaw, "Cracks in the Edifice").
27. I have drawn on N. Gregson Davis to translate "Au bout du petit matin". Davis attributes his translation to Derek Walcott: "I owe my serendipitous solution to the genius of Caribbean Nobel laureate Derek Walcott, who, in the context of an insightful essay on Patrick Chamoiseau's pathbreaking novel *Texaco*, employs the

term 'foreday morning' to render the term *petit matin* in passing reference to *Cahier*." See Davis, "Translator's Preface", xv.

28. "Au bout du petit matin bourgeonnant d'anses frêles les Antilles qui ont faim, les Antilles grêlées de petite vérole, les Antilles dynamitées d'alcool, échouées dans la boue de cette baie, dans la poussière de cette ville sinistrement échouées." I have used Davis's English translation of the French cited here.

29. Although the word *nègre* has been justifiably translated here as "nigger" or "negro" I have retained the French "nègre" since I believe it captures the shame he feels confronted with this image and the distance he wishes to create. Leaving the word in French in my opinion has a similar distancing effect when placed in an English sentence.

30. *Pongo*: I have retained the word used for a "great ape".

31. In Baudelaire's poem the bird, the albatross, is king of the skies but once he lands on the deck of the ship, the sailors, like the women in the streetcar, make fun of the bird for their own amusement: "This voyager, how awkward and weak! / Once so handsome, now comical and ugly." But in the Baudelaire poem, unlike in the *Cahier*, the poet immediately identifies with the mocked bird.

32. Jennings, *Escape from Vichy*, 8, 7.

33. Ibid., 142.

34. Ibid., 174–75.

35. Ibid., 181.

36. See Arnold, *Modernism*, 16, where he states: "André Breton . . . deserves much credit for having given Césaire to the larger world of letters."

37. Jennings, *Escape from Vichy*, 185.

38. As quoted ibid., 186.

39. Césaire: "Cette rencontre a été celle qui a orienté ma vie de manière décisive et je dois dire que son image, depuis, n'a cessé de m'accompagner." See Toumson and Henry-Valmore, *Aimé Césaire*, 100.

40. Jennings, *Escape from Vichy*, 200.
41. Ibid., 202.
42. See Linsley, "Wifredo Lam".
43. I have used Davis's translation, which perfectly retains the rhythm of the lines in Césaire's original.
44. See Arnold, *Modernism*, 17.
45. See Jules-Rosette, "Jean-Paul Sartre".
46. See Toumson and Henry-Valmore, *Aimé Césaire*, 108.
47. See Maximin, *Le Grand Camouflage*.
48. Curtius, "Cannibalizing *Doudouisme*", 515, 517.
49. For more on this see Rabbitt, "History into Story", 3.
50. See Toumson and Henry-Valmore, *Aimé Césaire*, 131.
51. "Nous constatons chez les membres du Parti Communiste Français: leur assimilationnisme invétéré; leur chauvinisme inconscient; leur conviction passablement primaire – qu'ils partagent avec les bourgeois européens – de la supériorité omnilaterale de l'Occident" (Midiohouan, *Aimé Césaire*, 138).
52. "Ce n'est ni le marxisme ni le communisme que je renie, que c'est l'usage que certains ont fait du marxisme et du communisme que je réprouve. Que ce que je veux, c'est que marxisme et communisme soient mis au service des peuples noirs, et non les peuples noirs au service du marxisme et du communisme" (ibid., 139–40).
53. See Toumson and Henry-Valmore, *Aimé Césaire*, 165.
54. Midiohouan, *Aimé Césaire*, 146, 149.
55. See Toumson and Henry-Valmore, *Aimé Césaire*, 165.
56. Kesteloot and Kotchy, *Aimé Césaire*, 235, 232.
57. See Toumson and Henry-Valmore, *Aimé Césaire*, 166.
58. Ibid., 175.
59. For more on this see Toumson and Henry-Valmore, *Aimé Césaire*, 176.
60. Childers, "Citizenship and Assimilation", 4.
61. Ibid., 7.

62. Toumson and Henry-Valmore, *Aimé Césaire*, 179.
63. See Reis's informative "'Territorial Diplomacy'", 67.
64. Daily, "Race, Citizenship", 357.
65. See Glissant, *Caribbean Discourse*. For an informative article on Glissant, see Ormerod, "Discourse and Dispossession".
66. Bernabé, Chamoiseau and Confiant, *Éloge de la créolité*, 18, 13.
67. See Glissant, "Aimé Césaire", 120–21.
68. Irele, "Introduction", 36
69. James Ferguson, "Aimé Césaire", *Guardian*, 20 April 2008, 3.
70. Glissant, "Aimé Césaire", 121.
71. In 2005 Césaire refused to meet with Nicolas Sarkozy, then minister of the interior, because of "le rôle positif" Sarkozy had attributed to colonialism in an article. The two men did eventually meet the following year, allowing Césaire to present Sarkozy with a copy of *Discours sur le colonialisme*.
72. Natalie Levisalles, "Nègre je suis, nègre je resterai", *Libération*, 18 April 2008.
73. *L'Express*, 1 June 2004.

BIBLIOGRAPHY

Arnold, A. James. *Modernism and Negritude: The Poetry and Poetics of Aimé Césaire*. Cambridge, MA: Harvard University Press, 1981.

Bernabé, Jean, Patrick Chamoiseau and Raphael Confiant. *Éloge de la créolité / In Praise of Creoleness*. Paris: Gallimard, 1990.

Césaire, Aimé. *Les armes miraculeuses*. Paris: Gallimard, 1946.

———. *Cadastre*. Paris: Éditions du Seuil, 1961.

———. *Cahier d'un retour au pays natal*. 1939. Reprint, Paris: Présence Africaine, 1983.

———. *Et les chiens se taisaient. Les armes miraculeuses*. Paris: Présence Africaine, 1956.

———. *Corps perdu*. Paris: Éditions du Seuil, 1949.

———. *Discours sur le colonialisme*. Paris: Présence Africaine, 1955.

———. *Ferrements*. Paris: Éditions du Seuil, 1960.

———. "Interview avec Aimé Césaire a Fort-de-France le 12 Janvier 1977". By Gérard George Pigeon. *Cahiers césairiens* 3 (1977): 1–6. https://digital.libraries.psu.edu/digital/collection/ces/id/106.

———. *Journal of a Homecoming / Cahier d'un retour au pays natal*. Translated by N. Gregson Davis; introduction, commentary and notes by F. Abiola Irele. Durham: Duke University Press, 2017.

———. *Lettre à Maurice Thorez*. Paris: Présence Africaine, 1956.

———. *moi, laminaire . . .* Paris: Éditions du Seuil, 1982.

———. "Poésie et connaissance". *Tropiques*, no. 12 (January 1945).

———. *Une saison au Congo*. Paris: Éditions du Seuil, 1966.

———. *Soleil cou coupé*. Reissued with *Corps perdu* in *Cadastre*. Paris: Éditions K, 1948.

———. *Une tempête*. Paris: Éditions du Seuil, 1969.

———. *La tragédie du roi Christophe*. Paris: Présence Africaine, 1963.

Childers, Kristen Stromberg. "Citizenship and Assimilation in Postwar Martinique: The Abolition of Slavery and the Politics of Commemoration". *Journal of the Western Society for French History* 34 (January 2006). http://hdl.handle.net/2027/spo.0642292.0034.018.

Curtius, Anny Dominique. "Cannibalizing *Doudouisme*, Conceptualizing the *Morne*: Suzanne Césaire's Caribbean Ecopoetics". *South Atlantic Quarterly* 115, no. 3 (July 2016): 513–34. https://french-italian.uiowa.edu/sites/french-italian.uiowa.edu/files/french-italian/Curtius_South%20Atlantic%20Quarterly%202016_513-34.pdf.

Daily, M. Andrew. "Race, Citizenship, and Antillean Student Activism in Postwar France, 1946–1968," *French Historical Studies* 37, no. 2 (Spring 2014): 331–57. https://doi.org/10.1215/00161071-2401629.

Davis, N. Gregson. "Translator's Preface". In *Journal of a Homecoming / Cahier d'un retour au pays natal*, by Aimé Césaire; translated by N. Gregson Davis; introduction, commentary and notes by F. Abiola Irele, xi–xviii. Durham: Duke University Press, 2017.

Delas, Daniel. *Aimé Césaire*. Paris: Hachette Supérieur, 1991.

Glissant, Édouard. "Aimé Césaire: The Poet's Passion". *Small Axe* 12, no. 3 (2008): 119–23. https://doi.org/10.1215/-12-3_27-119.

———. *Caribbean Discourse: Selected Essays*. translated by J. Michael Dash. Charlottesville: University Press of Virginia, 1989.

Irele, F. Abiola. "Introduction". In *Journal of a Homecoming / Cahier d'un retour au pays natal*, by Aimé Césaire; translated by N. Gregson Davis; introduction, commentary and notes by F. Abiola Irele, 1–73. Durham: Duke University Press, 2017.

Jennings, Eric T. *Escape from Vichy: The Refugee Exodus to the French Caribbean*. Cambridge, MA: Harvard University Press, 2018.

Jules-Rosette, Bennetta. "Jean-Paul Sartre and the Philosophy of Negritude: Race, Self, and Society". *Theory and Society* 36, no. 3 (June 2007): 265–85. www.jstor.org/stable/20730796.

Kesteloot, Lilyan, and Barthélemy Kotchy. *Aimé Césaire, l'homme et l'oeuvre*. Paris: Présence Africaine, 1973.

Linsley, Robert. "Wifredo Lam: Painter of Negritude". *Art History* 11 (December 1988): 527–44. https://doi.org/10.1111/j.1467-8365.1988 .tb00322.x.

Maximin, Daniel. *Le grand camouflage: Écrits de dissidence (1941–1945)*. Paris: Éditions Seuil, 2015.

Midiohouan, Guy Ossito, ed. *Aimé Césaire pour aujourd'hui et pour demain: Anthologie*. Saint-Maur: Éditions Sépia, 1995.

Nesbitt, Nick. "Departmentalization and the Logic of Decolonization". *L'Esprit Créateur* 47, no. 1 (July 2007): 32–43. https://www.jstor.org/ stable/26289302.

Ormerod, Beverly. "Discourse and Dispossession: Edouard Glissant's Image of Contemporary Martinique". *Caribbean Quarterly* 27, no. 4 (December 1981): 1–12. https://www.jstor.org/stable/40653423.

Rabbitt, K.M. "History into Story: Suzanne Césaire, Lafcadio Hearn, and Representations of the 1848 Martinique Slave Revolts". *Anthurium: A Caribbean Studies Journal* 12, no. 2 (December 2015): 3. http://doi .org/10.33596/anth.291.

Reis, Michele. "The 'Territorial Diplomacy' of the French Overseas Departments vis-à-vis the English-Speaking Caribbean". *Caribbean Journal of International Relations and Diplomacy* 1, no. 1 (June 2013): 65–73. https://journals.sta.uwi.edu/iir/index.asp?action=fullText PermaLink&articleId=382&galleyId=332.

Rosemont, Franklin, and Robin D.G. Kelley. *Black, Brown, and Beige: Surrealist Writings from Africa and the Diaspora*. Austin: University of Texas Press, 2009.

Sartre, Jean-Paul, and John MacCombie. "Black Orpheus". *Massachusetts Review* 6, no. 1 (Autumn 1964–Winter 1965). www.jstor.org /stable/25087216.

Sharpley-Whiting, T. Denean. *Negritude Women*. Minnesota: University of Minnesota Press, 2002.

Toumson, Roger, and Simonne Henry-Valmore. *Aimé Césaire: Le nègre inconsolé*. Fort-de-France: Vents des îles, 1993.

Walcott-Hackshaw, Elizabeth. "Cracks in the Edifice: Notes of a Native Daughter". Professorial lecture, University of the West Indies, St Augustine, Trinidad and Tobago, 19 April 2018.

ACKNOWLEDGEMENTS

Thank you, Shivaun and Funso, for your encouragement and the desire to include our Martinican family in this series. I must also thank my family for their support and the invaluable assistance of Anna Walcott-Hardy and Amy Hackshaw. I also am very fortunate to have generous scholars like Bridget Brereton who have always been willing to share their knowledge.